Glenhill Farm

THE HISTORY OF A FAMILY ESTATE

*As Revealed in the Correspondence between Brognard
Okie and Ernst and Mary Behrend*

BY RICHARD L. HART

With a Foreword by James B. Garrison

Published by Penn State Erie, the Behrend College, Erie, Pennsylvania

Contents

Foreword

Residential design and construction projects bring out the personalities of all those involved; thus projects from the past can tell us about the times, designers, clients, and constructors. Many Frank Lloyd Wright clients have written about their experiences with the architect and his idiosyncratic buildings. Richard Hart shines new light on the working process of R. Brognard Okie, a prolific early twentieth-century architect from Philadelphia, as documented in the correspondence related to Glenhill, a grand country estate near Erie, Pennsylvania. Even more compelling is the story of Ernst Behrend and his wife, Mary, Okie's clients. The Pennsylvania State Archives contains thousands of letters and drawings from the architect's office spanning a fifty-year period and covering many projects, but this one is especially well documented. In an era characterized by intensive letter writing, the clients' and architect's correspondence about even the most mundane items tells a story of a project conceived and constructed during the Great Depression and deeply affected by it.

The estate forms the core of the Penn State Erie campus, and Mr. Hart's long tenure there has given him a special feel for the place and its historical figures. Passages from the vast body of correspondence among all the major persons involved in the design and construction help tell the story of the selection of the architect, the design and construction processes, and no less important, life at the estate. It is an interesting window into a period when new money from industry—in this case, the Hammermill Paper Company—supported lavish lifestyles. The Great Depression affected even some of these fortunes, including the one amassed by Ernst and Mary Behrend.

Okie was fortunate to have a wealthy clientele that included the DuPonts, the Pews of Sun Oil, and others whose plans for large country estates went on throughout the 1920s and 1930s. These persons were discerning and demanding clients, and Okie served them well while also maintaining his own high standards for design and construction. Even in a somewhat diminished final state from its original conception, Glenhill stands with his best work of the decade and remains an architectural treasure in Northwestern Pennsylvania.

Starting with a dramatic site that overlooked Lake Erie in the distance, Okie and his clients transformed a motley collection of farm buildings into a cohesive gentleman's farm, complete with modern conveniences inside and out, including a new garage for Ernst Behrend's Duesenberg and other cars. The tragic death of the Behrends' son shortly before the design was started resulted in a family chapel modeled after Okie's own church, the original 1715 building for St. David's Church near his home in Newtown Square.

Not since the novelist Joseph Hergesheimer wrote about his own experience with Okie in 1925 in *From an Old House* have the words of Okie and his clients been so thoroughly examined for the multilayered stories that make up a design and construction project. The writer Hergesheimer viewed the events through a more romantic lens than the Behrends, even when the architect's decisions added cost to the project, but both clients shared an appreciation for the thoughtfulness of the design process. The overwhelming messages that come through from the clients' and architect's correspondence is a reverence for high-quality natural materials and careful, well-constructed details and the way history can pervade a contemporary dwelling. As a designer, Okie was aware of all the different languages of architectural design, from traditional to modern, but he chose the former to marry his work to the heritage of the land and people of the regions where he worked.

Glenhill is more than the story of a single project, letting us experience a process through the eyes of different personalities who come alive in the letters that bring nuance and life to an inanimate structure.

James B. Garrison

Preface

As the director of a college library that houses a collection of archival materials related to the Behrend family and the Hammermill Paper Company, it was a revelation to learn—more than a decade ago—that a large number of letters written by Ernst and Mary Behrend were held in the R. Brognard Okie file in the Pennsylvania State Archives. Furthermore, the fact that these letters were related to the construction of the Behrends' home, Glenhill Farm, which since 1948 has served as the campus of Penn State Erie, made this discovery even more compelling. The early history of the various buildings that constituted the Behrend estate and serve as the college's geographic core has remained largely unknown. A study leave from Penn State University in 2015 provided the time necessary to undertake a closer investigation of the letters and other materials pertaining to Glenhill. Some of that history is revealed in the pages that follow.

Introduction

A visitor strolling the campus of Penn State Erie, the Behrend College, will come upon a large fieldstone house with white clapboard trim. The house looks like it has been there a long time, and surrounded as it is with mature trees and attractive shrubs, it presents a pastoral setting regardless of the season. On closer inspection, the visitor may notice how the house seems to rest peacefully in the landscape as well as other features such as the antique wrought-iron hardware on the doors and windows, the oversized stone chimneys, and the unusual dormers and rain gutters. Nearby are other smaller fieldstone buildings of similar construction and two wooden barns. As a group, the buildings suggest that many years ago, this property was not a college but a prosperous farm.

The beautiful campus and its fieldstone buildings enjoy a unique history. While it did serve as a working farm, the owners of these buildings were not a typical farmer and his wife. On the contrary, Ernst and Mary Behrend were not really farmers at all; they were extremely successful industrialists and entrepreneurs who decided to build a country estate that would look like a historic farm. In doing so, they engaged a Philadelphia architect. His name was Brognard Okie, and this story of the architect and his clients is one that provides a glimpse into the lives of a prominent family at a stressful time, regarding not only their family events but also the nation's history as the Great Depression unfolded. Ultimately, the Behrends' gift of their estate to Penn State University in 1948 must be viewed not only as a wonderful gesture to promote higher education but also as a means of preserving an architecturally important house and its surrounding outbuildings.

Glenhill Farmhouse, east facade. This photograph presents a view of the residence as one approaches from the main entrance. (Photograph by John Fontecchio.)

Between 1932 and 1934, Brognard Okie designed and supervised the construction of a new home for Ernst and Mary Behrend in Harborcreek Township near Erie, Pennsylvania. Okie was an acclaimed architect when the Behrends hired him, known for his traditional houses, many of fieldstone and clapboard construction, primarily in the Philadelphia area. In the intervening years, Okie's reputation has remained strong, perhaps even grown, as documented in recent books and articles devoted to his work (Garrison 2013; Richie, Milner, and Huber 2005; Dixon 2010). His houses have remained popular and sought after. To this day, when Okie-designed homes come up for sale in Chester, Montgomery, and Delaware Counties in Southeastern Pennsylvania, realtors are quick to let prospective buyers know that Brognard Okie was the architect (Dixon 2010).

In designing and building what became known as Glenhill Farm, Okie exchanged numerous letters with Mr. Behrend, Mrs. Behrend, and their various secretaries and personal assistants. These letters, part of the R. Brognard Okie Architectural Papers, are housed in the Pennsylvania State Archives in Harrisburg. This is a voluminous collection, consisting of the historical office files of Okie, in which can be found documents relating to his various clients, including letters, telegrams, sketches, blueprints, vendor catalogs, photographs, and more.

The intent of this study is to document the early history of Glenhill Farm as it is revealed in the letters and other documents found in the Okie archives collection. Primarily a social history, it shares common ground with several other publications. This study provides new information on the background of the historic buildings of Penn State Erie and, as such, may be of interest to students of the college's history. However, the reader looking for a more comprehensive history of the estate and the college is referred to Benjamin A. Lane's book *Behrend Remembered: A Half Century of Penn State in Erie*. Similarly, while this study makes reference to many of the architectural features of an Okie-designed house, it is not an architectural history. Authoritative information on that subject can be found in *Stone Houses: Traditional Homes of R. Brognard Okie* by the leading Okie scholar James B. Garrison. Not only does Garrison present beautiful photographs, descriptions, and scholarly insight in regard to Okie-designed houses; he also provides background on the architect

View of the north facade. (Photograph by the author.)

View from the southwest. (Photograph by the author.)

Looking north from the southeast corner. (Photograph by RFrank Photography.)

The large barn, east side. (Courtesy Penn State Behrend Archives.)

and some of his clients. Finally, while this study describes the process of designing and building a home by Okie, a much more personal, firsthand account was published many years ago when the highly popular novelist Joseph Hergesheimer of West Chester, Pennsylvania, artfully recounted his experience in working with the architect on his old stone house in a 1925 memoir. The present study adds new information that complements these existing works.

THE BEHREND FAMILY

Ernst Behrend, along with his father, Moritz, and his brother, Otto, founded the Hammermill Paper Company in 1898. Born in 1869, Ernst was thirty-two years old when he became president of the new company in 1901. He had emigrated from Germany, where the family had a significant history of involvement in the paper-making business. All were well educated and skilled in modern manufacturing processes. Not only did Ernst have a university education; he had served as a lieutenant in the Prussian Mounted Artillery, and riding horses remained a lifelong interest. Ernst was clearly the key figure in the company, serving as president of Hammermill for nearly forty years (Ingold 2009).

In 1907, Ernst married Mary Brownell from a well-to-do Rhode Island family. Brownell, an accomplished sportswoman, had been the Rhode Island women's golf champion in 1902. A son, Warren, was born in 1909,

Ernst Behrend. (Courtesy Penn State   Mary Behrend. (Courtesy Penn State
Behrend Archives.)   Behrend Archives.)

and a daughter, Harriet, followed in 1911 (Ingold 2009). Interestingly, Harriet inherited both her mother's golfing talents and her father's interest in riding horses, as she would excel at both pursuits in later years.

Under the leadership of Ernst Behrend, over the course of more than three decades, the Hammermill Paper Company grew and prospered. Ernst was an innovator in several areas. A host of technological advancements were directly related to the company's success, including the invention of a system of high-speed watermarking. The development of a unique system of franchised sales agents combined with national advertising campaigns was another key to the company's success. Ernst became known for his advances in the area of employee relations. He pioneered "paid vacations and bonuses for hourly workers as well as sick and accident benefits, and in developing profit-sharing plans. Their employee magazine, the *Hammermill Bond*, was one of the first in the country, having published its inaugural issue in 1917" (Ingold 2010, 2). Ernst was one of the founding members of the National Industrial Conference Board in 1915, which later became known as the Conference Board (Ingold 2009, 1).

Mary Behrend played an integral role in the life of the company. Years later, she reflected on their life together—how they had lived on the grounds of the paper plant after their marriage, how Ernst sought her opinion and counsel, and how she and her husband devoted great personal effort to the success of the company. She was particularly involved in personnel decisions. She wrote,

> For example, if a new person of any importance was being considered as an employee for Hammermill, my husband would first discuss him with me and then very likely ask him to luncheon or dinner or possibly even to stay at the house overnight so that I might become acquainted with him. My husband always liked to bring his Mill problems home for discussion and wanted to hear my opinions concerning them. Many evenings we sat before the fire carefully going over these problems. I devoted a great deal of my time to the interests of the business and to entertaining Hammermill business connections. . . . Even when we travelled together, whether in England, on the continent, in India, the East or West Indies, Africa or the Orient, we always made contacts with the various Hammermill agents. (M. Behrend 1943, 1–2)[1]

For twenty-five years, the Behrends lived in the large brick home on the grounds of the Hammermill Paper Company on the shores of Lake Erie. The company followed the European practice, whereby the owner and key managers lived in homes on the grounds of the plant (Lane 1998, 16). Ernst and Mary lived comfortably. Profits were large enough to allow the Behrends to build a summer home in Newport, Rhode Island, in 1913 (M. Behrend 1943, 6). By the early 1920s, the company had more than a thousand employees, and profits exceeded $1 million annually (McQuillen and Garvey 1985, 69–77). In his history of the Behrend family, Benjamin A. Lane writes that "life at Hammermill House was assuredly grand, but by the mid-twenties, the Behrends apparently began to think about building another residence" (Lane 1998, 21).

In preparation for building an estate, the Behrends purchased several farms and other adjacent properties about three miles inland from Lake Erie southeast of the paper mill on land that rises to a height of several hundred feet in elevation above the lake. As Mrs. Behrend described it years later,

Schilling House. This is the site of what would become the location of the Glenhill residence. Hardly a renovation, Glenhill was essentially new construction. This photograph dates from 1931 or 1932 and shows Mary Behrend and farm superintendent Roy Bliley prior to the demolition of the Schilling House, one of the properties the Behrends had purchased to form the estate. (Courtesy Penn State Behrend Archives.)

> In 1931 my husband bought about 220 acres of land in Harborcreek Township, Erie County, and in the next two years he purchased various adjacent lots aggregating about 200 acres. Construction of a 23 room residence, swimming pool, garage, stable, bridle paths, etc., was begun in 1931 or 1932 and, in the main, completed in 1934. (M. Behrend 1943, 3)

Both of the Behrend children played a role in Okie's designs. When the story of Glenhill Farm begins in late 1931, daughter Harriet was a student at Vassar College. It is clear from the letters that Harriet was included in the planning process and that Mrs. Behrend was interested in seeing not only that suitable rooms were designed for her daughter but also that accommodations were included for friends who might be invited to visit. Son

Warren was involved for most unfortunate reasons. In 1929, the Behrends suffered a family tragedy when Warren, age twenty, died in an automobile accident in North Carolina while traveling to join the family, who were on their new yacht at anchor in Charleston, South Carolina. Although Warren was deceased by the time the Behrends proceeded to build their estate, his influence served to make the Behrend-Okie relationship most unusual from an architectural perspective. Okie designed a series of buildings for the Behrends, but the one that sets it apart from his other projects is the chapel in the nearby Wintergreen Gorge Cemetery that was built as a memorial to Warren and would come to serve as the family burial site.

Ernst and Mary Behrend were certainly unique among Okie's clients in terms of their geographic location. Living in the northwest corner of Pennsylvania, they were about as far from the architect's home base as they could be while still remaining in the same state. However, as the principal owners of the Hammermill Paper Company, the Behrends were quite typical of Okie's clients, among them key industrialists, politicians, bankers, and civic leaders.

As might be expected, the letters between the Behrends and Okie reveal much about issues that would be of concern to any home builder, including what to build, style of the building, specific design issues and room layouts, selection of materials, resolution of construction questions and problems, and cost. In addition, several other themes or specific anecdotes emerge. The letters show how Okie interacted with Mr. and Mrs. Behrend—how they communicated and what their various priorities and concerns were. The selection of Brognard Okie as the architect is a topic of interest, since it was not a straightforward process, and it involved several noteworthy individuals of national prominence. Among Okie's residential clients, the Behrends are believed to be the only ones for whom he designed a chapel, and details of that history are made known in the correspondence. The letters reveal some of the issues of the day, such as the interest in Colonial Revival architecture and themes related to the Great Depression, as a variety of the letter writers make reference to the difficult economic times. Finally, throughout the letters, the reader gets a sense of the thoughts and feelings of a unique family and a unique architect.

In addition to having a chapel built, Ernst and Mary Behrend stood apart from Okie's clients for other reasons. Their remote location in Erie seems to have had a direct impact on Okie's customary practices. Normally the architect would have made more site visits, but the long trip from Philadelphia made this more of a challenge. In addition, Okie made "an unusual number of drawings" for his client. This was probably because the originally intended main residence was never built and the Behrends changed their minds on several key matters, so many of the drawings went unused. In a letter to Mr. Behrend on March 22, 1935, Okie touched on both of these notions in one sentence as he discussed the details of his final bill:

> We feel that some concession should be made on our part for not giving the construction at the house as much supervision as we prefer giving our work as far as the number of trips to the building are concerned, but to offset this there were an unusual number of drawings made for the work in connection with the house, which of course involved quite a little drafting expense. (Okie Papers)[2]

This probably helps explain why the Behrend file in the archival collections is by far the largest among Okie's clients, both in terms of the correspondence section and in terms of the number of architectural drawings.

The Behrend correspondence is found in four manuscript boxes that are composed of two full boxes and two partial boxes. No other client is represented by more than one full box and one partial box. It is estimated that there are more than 1,500 letters in the Okie-Behrend file; many of these are detail-oriented messages between Okie and the local Erie contractors—particularly the Sessinghaus and Ostergaard firm, who built the main residence. If the architect and clients had been in closer proximity, some of the issues raised in these letters might have been resolved in person. There are 537 items in the Behrends' "Architectural Drawings" file, including elevations and blueprints; only one other client has more than 400 drawings, and only a handful have more than 150 drawings. Other primary sources for this study include materials from the Penn State Behrend

R. Brognard Okie. (Courtesy Pennsylvania State Archives.)

Archives, including oral history materials, early photographs, maps of the property, and Behrend family correspondence.

RICHARDSON BROGNARD OKIE JR.

At the time of his initial employment with the Behrends, Richardson Brognard Okie Jr. was fifty-six years old and had been an architect for more than three decades. Born in 1875 in Camden, New Jersey, Okie resided for most of his life in suburban Philadelphia. He received his secondary education at the West Chester Normal School in West Chester, Pennsylvania, and attended Haverford College for two years before graduating with a bachelor's degree from the architecture program at the University of Pennsylvania in 1897. For twenty years he worked in Philadelphia with H. Louis Duhring and Carl Ziegler in the Duhring, Okie & Ziegler firm. Their work was primarily residential in nature, and in architectural terms, the firm "had expressed a versatility with style, while staying within the popular Cotswold mixed with Pennsylvania farmhouse trend" (Tatman 2018). As early as 1912, the firm had been praised in a leading architectural journal for their designs of the "old colonial farm type" of Pennsylvania house (*Architectural Record* 1932, 307).

In 1918, Okie went into practice for himself, concentrating on his own specialties, which included the restoration, renovation, and new construction of the Pennsylvania colonial style, particularly the Pennsylvania farmhouse (Tatman 2018). In his book *Stone Houses: Traditional Homes of R. Brognard Okie*, James B. Garrison writes that Okie's work was rooted in colonial influences and that his "building forms were based on the traditional rural architecture of southeastern Pennsylvania, southern New Jersey, and the eastern shore of the Chesapeake Bay" (Garrison 2013, 17–18). Furthermore, Garrison notes that Okie's interest "was in the rural vernacular instead of high style city or country houses." He continues, "I don't really think it was romantic or nostalgic, but rather an appreciation for the strong architectural forms of that architecture as opposed to the more highly decorated high styles" (Garrison 2016). The majority of Okie's homes were made of fieldstone and wood in a most attractive style designed to invoke a time gone by. His office was at 306 South Smedley Street in Philadelphia, where he employed a small staff composed of a draftsman and his brother, William, who served as second in command and assisted him on projects, including Glenhill Farm (Garrison 2013, 18).

NOTES

1 Several years after Ernst Behrend's death, the estate taxes were being scrutinized by the Internal Revenue Service. That inquiry served as the rationale for this explanatory letter, written by Mrs. Behrend and her attorneys in 1943, in which she reflects on the family history.

2 In the interest of economy, "Okie Papers" is used to refer to the R. Brognard Okie Architectural Papers, "Correspondence, 1900–1948, 1959," MG-303, series 303m.1, Pennsylvania State Archives, Harrisburg, PA. Author, recipient, title of document (if applicable), and date of correspondence or document are provided in the citation only when not provided in the accompanying text.

First Correspondence

Hiring an Architect

In the fall of 1931, Spencer Gordon of Erie, Pennsylvania, was in the final stages of completing a task that his boss had given to him—finding an architect who could build a house and additional buildings that would serve as a new home. His boss, Ernst Behrend, age sixty-two, was a man of considerable wealth. His standards were extremely high; he was known to demand nothing but the best. Not just any architect would do.

By December, Gordon had made his choice. He had settled on Brognard Okie of Philadelphia to be responsible for the design of the Behrend family's new estate—for this was not merely a house; rather, this was to be a four-hundred-acre working farm with a large staff. Not only would new buildings be constructed, but several existing houses and garages would be modified. Accommodations were needed for numerous animals including horses, sheep, goats, and dogs; garage space was required for at least eight vehicles; and living quarters had to be designed not only for the Behrend family but also for the farm manager and his family, the butler, the maid, the cook, the chauffeurs, and the personal assistant to Mr. Behrend.

However, there was a problem. Although Gordon was convinced that Okie was the best architect for the job, it was clear that Mr. Behrend had serious reservations. An undated letter to the architect from Gordon begins as follows:

Dear Mr. Okie,

A letter from Mr. Behrend received by air mail today reflects again his perturbation with respect to your engineering ability and the practicability of
your house designs. He seems anxious lest my enthusiasm carry me to the
point of involving you or rather putting you in his debt beyond the sum
arranged upon in New York. It is probable that I have done this as far as
the model goes and with respect to the barn and Schilling house measure-
ments. (Okie Papers)

This interesting letter goes on for five handwritten pages and, although
undated, looks to be the first letter in the correspondence—most likely
written in November or December 1931. It is clear that Gordon speaks for
Mr. Behrend, and in fact, the letter is written on Mr. Behrend's personal
letterhead that reads "Ernst R. Behrend, President, Hammermill Paper
Company." Gordon provides some insight into the role that he plays for
Mr. Behrend and perhaps the kind of trouble that can afflict the wealthy:

Every now and again some cunning person with an ax to grind or some
prejudiced and ignorant person gets to Mr. Behrend and influences him
very much until we get at the facts. . . . This is one of the reasons he has
me with him now. (Okie Papers)

It is not immediately obvious from the correspondence or other documents, but it turns out that Gordon had studied architecture, and although
not a practicing architect, he shared Okie's alma mater—having graduated
from the School of Architecture at the University of Pennsylvania in 1913
(Architectural Alumni Society 1934). Perhaps this connection helps explain
Gordon's enthusiastic endorsement of Okie to the Behrends or perhaps
during his student days, he acquired a special appreciation of the traditional Pennsylvania farmhouses and outbuildings, which he might have
encountered in the Philadelphia area. In any event, Gordon was eager to
see that the Behrends hire Okie.

It is evident from the early letter that Gordon and Okie had met previously in person and that they met in New York City. It is not clear if either

Ernst or Mary Behrend were involved in that meeting. It seems that as part of his selection process, Gordon had requested and received preliminary drawings from Okie. In the letter, Gordon refers to house plans, submitted by Okie, that have been reviewed by the family, and in fact, he notes that the Behrends' daughter, Harriet, "seemed to like the plans very much indeed." He also refers to a model that Okie is constructing. The main theme of the letter is that Gordon intends to convince Mr. Behrend that Okie is the right man for the job, but he needs Okie's assistance. The letter continues:

> Arm me with letters from folks who have lived in your houses one year and more who will hit this matter of a) comfort b) convenience c) efficiency of heating plant, plumbing, etc. on the head. (Okie Papers)

Okie and Gordon must have discussed securing letters of reference from other clients when they met in person, since Gordon identifies two possible letter writers that sound good to him in "Mr. Hergesheimer" and the "Baldwin Locomotive man": "Four or five really well done letters should do the trick." Gordon also asks for a "house scheme with some 'foxy' pencil elevations and an interior suggestion or two." Finally, Okie's fees are mentioned several times, and it is clear that Gordon has asked Okie for more drawings and plans than had been originally agreed to and that if Okie is not chosen for the project, he will be out of luck in regard to payment, since Mr. Behrend is not inclined to pay "beyond the sum arranged." Apparently Gordon is overstepping the bounds of what his employer intended. In another letter, dated December 21, Gordon again confirms his interest in Okie and indicates that he would like the three of them to meet in New York in early January 1932 at the Hotel Barclay (Okie Papers).

On December 31, 1931, in his first letter in regard to the Behrend account, addressed to Spencer Gordon, Okie provides a list of twenty-eight former or current clients for consideration as references. Nowhere in the letter does Okie show any sign that he takes umbrage at the fact that Mr. Behrend has questioned whether his skills and abilities are up to the task of building a suitable house for him in Erie. On the contrary, his tone is even tempered as he writes,

Mr. Behrend will very likely know quite a number of the people whose names I am giving you and could get from them an expression of opinion as to whether or not they were satisfied with the work we did, etc. (Okie Papers)

To today's reader, some of these names, such as Pew and DuPont, may suggest the exalted social and economic strata occupied by many of Okie's clients. If those names don't resonate with some, then certainly the *titles* of "Chief Justice Owen J. Roberts" and "Governor C. Douglass Buck" provide further indication of the elite standing of Okie's clients. (Note: Okie mistakenly refers to Associate Justice Roberts of the United States Supreme Court as "Chief Justice.")

There is no indication in the correspondence that Mr. Behrend had a personal acquaintance with any of the men or women suggested by Okie. However, he certainly must have been familiar with some of their names. For example, Joseph N. Pew Jr. had served as president of Sun Oil since 1916 and would later be appointed chairman of the board. Today he is remembered as a founder of the Pew Charitable Trusts. Another client, C. Douglass Buck, governor of Delaware for two years at the time Okie listed him as a reference, would go on to serve as a two-term senator from the state (*New York Times* 1965). His wife, Alice, was a member of the DuPont family, and their home, called Buena Vista, which had been altered and added to by Okie, was located in New Castle, Delaware.

A third client, of whom Mr. Behrend might have been aware, was the "Mr. Hergesheimer" who Gordon had referred to in the first letter. Joseph Hergesheimer of West Chester was a novelist of considerable acclaim. Hergesheimer's house, named the Dower House, is the oldest home in West Chester, Chester County. Dating to 1712, it was renovated and greatly enlarged by Okie in the early 1920s. Hergesheimer had described the renovation process in a memoir, *From an Old House*, that was published by Alfred A. Knopf, a fascinating book that conveys not only details about the process of renovation but also the deep affection and interest that he and Okie shared in regard to early American homes.

While Spencer Gordon had asked Okie for "four or five" letters of reference, only three are found in the archives. The letters are from Samuel M.

Vauclain, Owen J. Roberts, and A. O. Leighton. All three letters were forwarded to Gordon by Okie, and in each case, Okie included a letter of his own to Gordon. In his letter to Gordon dated April 6, 1932, which accompanied the letter of reference from Owen J. Roberts, Okie wrote,

> It would be possible to get a great many more letters of the same kind but, including the enclosed, you have received letters from three of the most prominent men for whom we have done work. (Okie Papers)

In addition, in another letter, Okie indicated that he was thankful for a "good word" from another reference:

> I went to the University to see Dr. Laird last week and to personally thank him for putting in a good word for us when you saw him in reference to an architect some time ago. (Okie Papers, February 11, 1932)

In this case, Okie is referring to Warren Powers Laird, dean of the School of Architecture at the University of Pennsylvania, whom Okie must have known since his college days. Dr. Laird had served on the architecture faculty since 1891, and by 1932 he was about to retire after a long career. Thus the Behrends received several letters from clients and a verbal reference from Dr. Laird in support of Okie.

It is likely that the Behrends recognized Samuel Vauclain's name when they read his letter to Spencer Gordon. Vauclain had spent his entire career with the Baldwin Locomotive Works of Philadelphia, one of the nation's largest companies. Skilled as a mechanical engineer and inventor, Vauclain had risen through the ranks to become president of the company. With an interest in politics, he had received active consideration as a presidential candidate at the 1920 Republican National Convention in Chicago (Brown 2000), and he appeared on the cover of *Time* magazine in 1923.

Vauclain's home, called Broadlawn, was on Philadelphia's "Main Line" in Rosemont, Delaware County, and Okie had designed it some thirty years earlier as a young architect. Vauclain writes that he has been informed by Okie of "the peculiar situation which has arisen." (This may suggest that Okie *had* taken umbrage at Ernst Behrend's "perturbation" and lack of trust in his qualifications, as noted earlier.) In this letter of four short paragraphs, Vauclain has nothing but praise for Okie in terms of his abilities as an architect and his personal qualities:

My dear Mr. Gordon:

I have been approached by Mr. Brognard Okie, an architect in the City, to give him a letter expressing therein my satisfaction and dis-satisfaction with a dwelling house he designed and supervised when under construction located at Bryn Mawr, Pennsylvania (Rosemont).

Mr. Okie has explained to me the peculiar situation which has arisen placing a question mark upon his ability as an architect to design a house not only artistic in itself but one in which to live is a perfect and continued delight. A little over thirty years ago I employed Mr. Okie as my architect. He was then a young man, and I being an engineer and designer (of locomotives) soon became impressed by his originality and modesty together with a willingness to at all times make any effort and any change in his design that might be suggested by the ladies of my family, et cetera.

This house has been a wonderful home all these years and there has been no desire on the part of any of my family, a member of which is also an architect of considerable repute, to make any modification. Convenience, simplicity, durability and a construction most pleasing to the eye, it stands today without depreciation.

Mr. Okie is not only an architect of distinction but a gentleman of taste and ability. Any work that might be entrusted to him for execution would, I am quite sure, when completed give perfect satisfaction, and no difficulties would arise to lessen the personal and professional relationship between him and his client. (March 21, 1932, Okie Papers)

The second letter of reference received by Gordon was dated April 5, 1932, and was authored by Owen J. Roberts, whose estate, known as Bryn Coed, was located in West Vincent Township, Chester County—about thirty miles west of Philadelphia. Like Vauclain, Roberts is brief in his remarks but nothing short of complimentary in respect to the work of the architect:

My dear Sir:

Mr. Okie has asked me to say to you what I care to respecting the farm house and barn alteration and extension he did for me in Chester County, Pa.

I might say that while I call it an alteration, the work was more new than alteration, since the new structure is about twice as large as the old building which was on the site.

We put ourselves unreservedly in Mr. Okie's hands and the first plans he submitted were so satisfactory that very slight changes were made.

The greatest care was shown in providing for our comfort and convenience. In the matter of the closet room, etc., the arrangements as originally submitted were more than adequate. As respects construction, Mr. Okie's requirements were very severe and the contractors were compelled to live up to them to the letter. As a consequence I think we have one of the best built and most substantial houses I know of.

I am so pleased with the result that I should be glad if you could sometime come to see the place. (Okie Papers)

The letter gives Roberts's address at the top of the letter as "Supreme Court of the United States, Washington, D.C." Roberts was fifty-six years old at the time and had served on the United States Supreme Court since his nomination by President Herbert Hoover in 1930. His national reputation dates back to 1924, when President Calvin Coolidge appointed him as special US attorney to investigate the "Teapot Dome" scandal that had taken place during the administration of the Coolidge's predecessor, Warren Harding (Cortner 2000). There can be little doubt that Spencer Gordon and the Behrends were aware of Roberts when they received his letter, and it is likely that they may have followed his accomplishments in subsequent years, as he went on to serve fifteen years on the Supreme Court, retiring in 1945. The estate at Bryn Coed (also referred to as the Strickland-Roberts Home) was added to the National Register of Historic Places in 1978 (National Register of Historic Places, n.d.).

A. O. Leighton was a partner in the construction firm of Irwin and Leighton of Philadelphia—perhaps the city's largest such firm at that time and responsible for buildings such as hospitals, railroad terminals, college buildings, and the Federal Reserve Bank of Philadelphia. In fact, the firm survives and thrives to this day in the same line of work (IrwinLeighton .com, n.d.). Leighton's home in Villanova had been completed two years earlier. In a lengthy letter of recommendation, he praised Okie's abilities. In an interesting passage, he described how, after more than two years of searching, he finally found the right architect:

> One Sunday afternoon I was out in the country with my wife and we came to a house well off the main road that was just being finished, and that embodied the spirit of things that we were after. It sat in the country side as if it belonged there. Unlike other houses we had looked at, it enhanced rather than detracted from the rural beauty around it. The trees, the grass and the stream took on added charm from being near it. The simplicity of its detail and the proportions of its masses of masonry and frame construction were a delight to the eye. . . . There was no one around, not even a watchman, and nothing to indicate the name of the architect, so I had to break the padlock on the construction office and obtain it from the plans filed there. The next day I saw Mr. Okie and he accepted the commission. (Leighton to Gordon, March 22, 1932, Okie Papers)

In spite of these glowing references, several factors were at work that jeopardized Okie's chances of getting the job. A letter from Gordon to Okie tells why:

> The bad news is this: Someone whom the Behrends had as guests spent a lot of time telling them how impractical you are. It seems that you can do a very attractive house . . . but they are very impractical from an engineering angle and some have been positively unlivable, and this person whose name is unknown to me, intimates that a great many of your clients had trouble ever since they moved into your house. This has disturbed the Behrends very much. (Okie Papers, n.d.)

To compound matters, a family tragedy occurred near the end of March within only a few days of receipt of the letters of reference. A telegram from Gordon to Okie relayed the news:

MR BEHRENDS BROTHER DIED TODAY STOP LEAVING TONIGHT
FOR BOSTON STOP APPRECIATE VERY MUCH YOUR SPLENDID HELP
STOP . . . WILL WRITE AFTER FUNERAL. (March 25, 1932, Okie Papers)

Bernard Behrend was an internationally known electrical engineer and
inventor. He committed suicide at his home in Boston, and his death was
a severe blow to his brother Ernst (Lane 1998, 10–11).

Nevertheless, a few weeks later the Behrends met with Okie in Philadelphia. At that meeting, he presented them with a three-dimensional
model of a proposed main residence. Apparently Okie thought that the
meeting was only a partial success. The Behrends were critical of some of
his plans and wanted to place the swimming pool in a location that he did
not support. As he wrote to Spencer Gordon,

> In some ways the meeting with Mr. and Mrs. Behrend on Saturday after-
> noon was very satisfactory but I was disappointed to learn from Mrs. Beh-
> rend that she preferred to adhere more closely to the plans that you had
> sketched in accordance with the suggestions. . . . Also, it seems to me the
> swimming pool will not work out so satisfactorily to the west as it would to
> the east of the house—particularly, as the swimming pool building would
> have to be on a decidedly higher level and we could not take advantage of
> the slope of the ground as we do in our present scheme. (April 12, 1932,
> Okie Papers)

However, the optimistic Gordon told Okie not to worry about such
details: "A little time will do many things. They are at least now fully sold
on Brognard Okie" (Okie Papers, n.d.). So in spite of the critical remarks
from the Behrends' guests and the distressing death of Bernard Behrend,
the strategies had been effective, and Mr. Behrend's reservations about
Okie had been overcome. By mid-April 1932, it is evident not only that
Brognard Okie had been granted the job but also that the Behrends were
eager to get the project under way.

CHAPTER TWO

Architect and Client

Making Plans and Decisions

HOW THEY COMMUNICATED

The planning and construction of Glenhill Farm was anything but a straightforward affair. Rather, plans were made, then changed, and frequently changed again. The process was an active one, albeit somewhat sporadic, over the course of more than three years. Between December 1931 and January 1936, communication between Brognard Okie and the Behrends was considerable, with 1932 through 1934 being the busiest.

This communication took a variety of forms. Okie maintained a comprehensive and detailed office file of his correspondence and architectural plans over the course of his private practice from 1918 to 1945. The Behrend-Okie correspondence takes the form of hundreds of letters supplemented by occasional Western Union telegrams. The most frequent correspondent is Brognard Okie, since the vast majority of communication from his office originated with him, although many letters were authored by his brother, William, or by his secretary.

At the Erie end, correspondence addressed to Okie, his brother, and his secretary was composed by a number of authors. While Mr. Behrend wrote to Okie, it is equally likely that one of his assistants or secretaries wrote for him. This list of names includes assistants Spencer Gordon and Frank Knauer and secretaries E. A. Ferguson, Joseph Chladek, and Louise Fratus. Mary Behrend was a frequent correspondent with both Brognard and William Okie.

The office files include many hundreds of letters between the architect and a considerable number of contractors and suppliers. These include the Erie firms of Henry Shenk, who built the chapel, and Sessinghaus and Ostergaard, who built the house, garage, shelter shed, and more; Henry Hipple of Harrisburg, Pennsylvania, who provided antique lumber and custom millwork such as windows and doors; and Myron Teller of Kingston, New York, one of the providers of the handmade, antique-era, wrought-iron hardware.

Of course, not all the communication was written. References to meetings and visits are found in the letters, and in that sense the correspondence gives an incomplete view of the issues and decisions. Throughout the letters, references are made to visits that both Brognard and William Okie made to Erie—probably a dozen or so. There may well have been more visits that are simply not mentioned in the correspondence. Meetings were also held in New York and Philadelphia. The Behrends were frequent travelers and made active use of the Hotel Barclay at Forty-Eighth Street and Lexington Avenue in New York City, and on several occasions, they requested that Okie meet them there. When in Philadelphia, they preferred the Ben Franklin Hotel on Chestnut Street, where they also met with the architect. In addition, they met at Okie's office in center city Philadelphia. The correspondence includes references to telephone calls between the Behrends and Okie; however, such references are extremely rare, and it appears that the old-fashioned letter was their primary means for discussing plans for the estate.

In regard to style and content, the letters of Brognard Okie, Ernst Behrend, and Mary Behrend are something of a curiosity and worthy of note in that they reveal personal qualities and interests of their authors. Brognard Okie's letters were, without fail, typewritten and in the form of a standard business letter. The identifying notation at the bottom of each ("EV") indicated that they were prepared for him by his secretary, Ethel Volkmar. Often Okie's letters were accompanied by sketches or blueprints for upcoming work. His style was formal but cordial. The letters were descriptive, using lengthy, well-written sentences. They often covered several topics and ran between one and three typewritten pages. They make good reading. James Garrison notes that the architect "was obviously very erudite and could communicate well" (Garrison 2013, 18). In Okie's letters, he seems to have been fastidious in making sure to address all previous questions that the Behrends had asked of him. In closing his letters to Mr. Behrend, he would usually write,

With kindest regards to Mrs. Behrend and yourself, I am

Very truly yours,
(signed) R. Brognard Okie

Mr. Behrend's letters were usually quite succinct. Sometimes they were only a few sentences in length. Often they dealt with technical issues such as plumbing or heating products. His letter from September 12, 1933, was only one sentence long. On his Hammermill Paper Company letterhead, in its entirety it reads,

Dear Mr. Okie:

What do you think of the General Electric humidifying and heating system for the addition at the farm?

Sincerely yours,
(signed) Ernst R. Behrend (Okie Papers)

Although the vast majority of Mr. Behrend's letters were typed by one of his secretaries, an occasional neatly handwritten letter appears in the file.

Whereas Mr. Behrend's handwriting is easy to read, Mrs. Behrend's can often be quite difficult to make out. Apparently Okie had trouble reading Mrs. Behrend's letters, since not long after the correspondence began, two versions of each of her letters started appearing in his office files—one in Mary's original longhand and one typed transcription, presumably by Okie's secretary.

Unlike her husband's letters, Mary Behrend had little to say in regard to technical issues. Rather, the questions that she raises have to do with the overall design and features of the house, the exterior appearance, and the layout of interior spaces. In the later years, her letters often

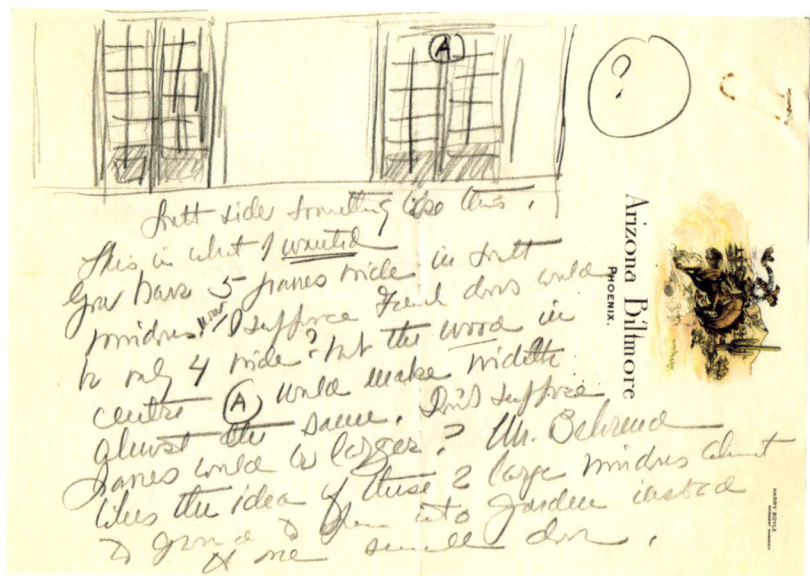

Letter to Okie from the Arizona Biltmore, 1933. It was not unusual for Mrs. Behrend to write letters on the stationery of a hotel where the Behrends were staying. Nor was it unusual for her to add diagrams to her letters. The penmanship could be challenging. In this letter, she made suggestions in regard to the design of the windows on the south side of the living room for the 1934 family wing addition. (Courtesy Pennsylvania State Archives.)

concerned issues related to the chapel in Wintergreen Gorge Cemetery. And while most of her letters were handwritten, others were typed. They appeared on a variety of letterheads including her own personal letterhead, Ernst's company president letterhead, and the letterhead of a variety of hotels where they may have been staying. Frequently, Mrs. Behrend included her own sketches of a floor plan or other aspect of the house, illustrating a suggestion that she wanted to propose to Okie in regard to the placement of or features within a room. Mrs. Behrend was something of an artist and painter, and some of the sketches that accompanied her letters were not without artistic skill.

CHOOSING A STYLE: THE PENNSYLVANIA FARMHOUSE
The early correspondence between Brognard Okie and Spencer Gordon provides a strong indication of the type and style of buildings and ambiance

that the Behrends were most interested in achieving. Gordon articulated the essence of it when he wrote a letter to the landscape architect whom the Behrends had retained, Dr. Arthur Cowell, with a copy to Okie:

> The Behrends have given considerable thought to the matter and are steadfast in their desire that this be a rustic, simple and unostentatious place, following, in general, the early Pennsylvania tradition as to the type of house, barns, out buildings, etc.
>
> It seems to me that this is very logical and fitting. Does not all this to some extent determine the landscape? Is it not our part to emphasize as reasonably as may be the picturesque quaintness of the farm tradition?
>
> I realize that we shall have to depart from this in such cases as the size and location of the manure pile, but in general, I think we can establish and keep to a simple quaintness, nevertheless. . . . Should not the whole setting down there have the effect of an early domestic Pennsylvania tradition? (February 1, 1932, Okie Papers)

The Behrends' interest in a house, barn, and outbuildings in the "early domestic" tradition is what today would be termed Colonial Revival architecture. In the early 1930s, there was widespread interest in homes built in a colonial style, which took many different forms, including the most popular—the Cape Cod—as well as the early American farmhouse, the Dutch Colonial, and the Greek Revival (Gebhard 1987, 145–46). Another popular style, and the category in which Glenhill Farm and other Okie homes fall, is the Pennsylvania farmhouse style.

National interest in colonial architecture was extremely strong in the 1920s and 1930s, and this interest can be traced to the Philadelphia Centennial Exposition of 1876 (Lanier and Herman 1997, 167). As Garrison notes, the exposition was an occasion for national retrospection, which promoted a romanticized view of the country's history (Garrison 2013, 14). The centennial celebration brought attention to the homes of the country's Founding Fathers and helped lead to Colonial Revival houses serving as the most dominant style from 1900 to 1940 (Dixon 2010, 75). Since the Centennial Exposition had been held in Philadelphia, it had been especially resonant with people in that area.

Interest in Colonial Revival architecture grew at this time as the result of other influences, including the publication and widespread circulation of new magazines that published articles, photographs, and drawings of new colonial-style houses. These magazines included such titles as *House and Garden*, *Town and Country*, *Country Life*, and *Better Homes and Gardens* (Gebhard 1987, 111). It is clear that Mrs. Behrend was acquainted with this genre of magazine, since the archives contain a number of clippings and articles from contemporary publications that she forwarded to Okie with comments expressing her attraction to various architectural features, both exterior and interior. For example, by means of a clipping showing a colonial house in the May 1932 issue of *House Beautiful*, Mrs. Behrend notes her interest in the picket fence, antique doors, and an overhang on the outside of the house.

At the same time, there was a growth in the number of books devoted to regional colonial architecture. In fact, Okie had written the introduction

Magazine illustration for Okie. Mrs. Behrend sent numerous clippings from magazines to Okie to illustrate design features that she liked, including this example from the May 1932 issue of *House Beautiful*. She pointed out the picket fence, suggested and drew an overhang (of which Okie disapproved), and proposed the purchase of used doors as a way to economize. (Courtesy Pennsylvania State Archives.)

to one such title, authored by his friend and fellow architect Eleanor Raymond. Published in 1931 and titled *Early Domestic Architecture of Pennsylvania*, the book provides a photographic record of early homes, barns, and outbuildings of Southeastern Pennsylvania—including the type from which Glenhill's inspiration comes. The correspondence indicates that Okie loaned this book to the Behrends and that it was extremely influential in their decisions regarding the design of the bathhouse, which was built near the swimming pool.

Restorations of colonial-era buildings provided further evidence of the national interest in colonial architecture and in the country's history and served to spur even wider interest. In 1926, Philadelphia hosted a Sesquicentennial Exposition, of which the centerpiece was the restoration of High Street—two blocks of colonial-era buildings. Okie was the chief architect (Garrison 2013, 36). That same year, work began on the restoration of Colonial Williamsburg, a project funded by John D. Rockefeller Jr., which would eventually be highly influential in further promoting the colonial revival (Gebhard 1987, 117). In the mid-1930s, Okie would be a key player in two much-publicized restoration projects. For both projects, he served as the lead architect. One was the restoration of the Betsy Ross House in Philadelphia; the other was the re-creation of Pennsbury Manor, the county estate of William Penn, located on the banks of the Delaware River in Bucks County. Although these projects were completed after his work on Glenhill Farm, they are highly indicative not only of the considerable and scholarly interest that Okie had in colonial architecture but also of the popular interest that existed for his re-creations of colonial buildings.

The correspondence suggests that the Behrends were interested in learning more about colonial Pennsylvania and sought Okie's assistance. He loaned them at least two books at this time, writing,

> Neither of these books are descriptive of Pennsylvania Dutch houses, but they each give a pretty good idea of the people, their method of living. . . . The Tales of Kloster, describes life at Ephrata before this most interesting settlement had started its decline. (Okie to Gordon, December 31, 1931, Okie Papers).[1]

The Pennsylvania farmhouse possessed several traits that were common to all styles of Colonial Revival domestic architecture. One important element was the "interpretive" nature of the house—that is, the revival design was not a copy of an original but rather an interpretation that borrowed "stylistic elements" from the originals (Lanier and Herman 1997, 167). Gordon's reference (quoted above) in regard to the "size and location of the manure pile" is indicative of this interpretive aspect. While the new estate would include a manure pile, Gordon seems to suggest that it certainly would not be close to the house as it might have been in colonial times. Also, the colonial revival house "was modified for modern living" by adding features like porches and patios and extensive windows, none of which were common to colonial-era design. All modern conveniences and new technology of bathrooms and kitchens were included. Finally, the buildings were more modest in scale than what had come before. The reduced size could be seen as a reaction to the budget limitations of the Depression years, but the trend was also symbolic and reflective of the era's sense of "modesty and reticence" (Gebhard 1987, 119).

WHAT TO BUILD: HOUSES, CHAPEL, GARAGES, AND MORE

Between December 1931 and April 1932, there was much activity in regard to planning the new estate. Okie had drawn up architectural plans and sketches, including revisions to his first attempts. Letters and telegrams had been exchanged between Okie and Spencer Gordon, and a meeting appears to have taken place in New York in early January at the Hotel Barclay with Gordon, the Behrends, and Okie in attendance. A landscape architect—Dr. Arthur Cowell—formerly a member of the faculty at the Pennsylvania State College (now Pennsylvania State University), had been engaged.

Okie visited the property in Erie several times in 1932, including at least twice that winter. On January 19, he wrote to Gordon, "I am going to try and arrange to leave here Friday night and spend Saturday in Erie with you" (Okie Papers). Two days later, Gordon replied by telegram, "MEETING PENNSYLVANIA TRAIN SATURDAY MORNING BRING HIKING BOOTS OR ARTICS" (January 21, 1932, Okie Papers). Presumably Okie

Early farm photograph. A scene such as this would have greeted Okie on one of his early visits to the property. Looking northward, the large barn is on the left. (Courtesy Penn State Behrend Archives.)

took the overnight Pennsylvania Railroad train from Philadelphia to Erie. Implicit in Gordon's telegram is acknowledgement of the fact that winter weather in Erie is typically much more severe in terms of snowfall and colder temperatures than Okie would be used to in Philadelphia, and he would need proper footwear to walk the property.

One of the most interesting documents in the office files is a memorandum that Okie must have written in the winter of 1932 shortly after his January visit to Erie, after having toured the property and likely consulted in depth with Mr. and Mrs. Behrend. This document of more than eleven typewritten pages is titled "Office Memorandum regarding Requirements for Residence of Mr. and Mrs. Ernst R. Behrend, Erie, Pennsylvania" (Okie 1932). In it, Okie lays out a description of some of the buildings that are to be built, including a detailed listing of key components of the main residence. It would have been a useful document for planning purposes and for sharing with the Behrends to make sure that all parties had a mutual understanding of what was desired. James Garrison notes that such a document between architect and client would have been quite unusual and may be evidence of yet another way in which the considerable distance between Erie and Philadelphia modified Okie's typical practice (Garrison 2017). More than any other document in the state archives, this memorandum gives the best indication of the Behrends' original vision and intentions regarding the design of their new estate. Rather expressively, it begins with Okie's description of the property:

> The site is on a ridge running approximately east and west, the top being woodland, with a rather abrupt slope to the north and lake, now under cultivation, a lowland in which a farm group is located, and distant wooded knolls between the farm and the lake. On the west side the property narrows, sloping slightly due west, slightly down and up southwest, to a sharp cliff bordering Wintergreen Gulch. . . . The woodland is mixed evergreen and deciduous material, with tall hardwoods predominating on the north side, and open glades affording alternative house sites, through which views of the lake can be obtained. (Okie 1932, 1)

In terms of the nature of the estate, Okie writes,

> The general requirements of the development are somewhat as follows: A residence . . . with semi-detached swimming pool; a garage, with quarters included; and a farm group. . . . The general character of the development is to be informal, probably of early-American inspiration, and is to suggest development over a long term of years with additions from time to time. In the design there are under consideration native stone work, stone or brick painted, and clapboards. (Okie 1932, 2)

These descriptions touch on several points of interest. First, the reference to the swimming pool is significant, since Mr. Behrend was an inveterate swimmer and having a pool close to the house was a matter of great importance to him (Lane 1998, 23). Second, mention of a "farm group" indicated that the Behrends intended this to be a working farm and that they had purchased eight adjoining properties (or portions thereof), including houses and barns, in order to form their estate. Some of the properties were working farms, so existing barns, stables, and such were already present on this combined property (Richardson 1932). Third, Okie noted that the design was "to suggest development over a long term of years with additions from time to time." Those who have studied Okie's work would point out that this phrase refers to one of the architect's trademarks, known as the "additive" or "narrative" nature of his houses: "His designs capture the additive character of early houses that had been incrementally expanded over time as owners became more prosperous" (Richie, Milner, and Huber 2005, 126). Using strategies such as different roof lines and perpendicular additions, the houses were made to look like additional wings or sections had been added in later years. James Garrison describes it this way: "He created narrative stories in his buildings that might suggest several phases of construction over time, even for new construction conducted in one campaign" (Garrison 2013, 18).

The majority of the memorandum is devoted to description and miscellaneous notes and observations regarding the residence, including the garage, which would provide housing for some of the servants. The house would include a living room designed as a library approximately twenty by thirty feet in dimension. The first floor of the house would also include a dining room, a sunroom, a breakfast room with space for plants and access to a terrace, a serving pantry, and "a sanctum which is to be Mr. Behrend's private retreat, something in the nature of a house office." A two-story "service wing" needed to include the kitchen and kitchen pantry on the first floor and various living quarters for the staff:

> A married couple, butler and wife, the wife possibly serving in one of the capacities noted below. One laundress; one maid; one cook; either two chauffeurs, or one chauffeur and one extra man who might also serve as chauffeur. Accommodations for these servants should be found on the first or second floor of the service wing and in connection with the garage. (Okie 1932, 4)

On the second floor would be found the suites for Mr. Behrend, Mrs. Behrend, and their daughter, Harriet. All would have a private bath and a sun porch or balcony. Of importance to Mr. Behrend was as much light and ventilation as possible—as Okie put it, "maximum fenestration"—and a large bathroom with all the amenities to which Mr. Behrend was accustomed. The women each required fireplaces and an "ample wardrobe," with Harriet's wardrobe "subdivided for riding clothes, day clothes, and evening clothes," reflecting her accomplishments as a highly regarded equestrian. The second floor requires two guest rooms, each with a private bath.

A section on "recreation features" describes the desired attributes of the swimming pool, including its size, ample walkway, protection from the weather, and nearby dressing rooms for men and women. A second recreation feature describes an area that is certainly intended for use by Harriet and her friends, including late-night use:

> A recreation room with fireplace, space for a Frigidaire, an electric plate, and such incidentals as would make this room attractive to a group of young people. The element of noise should have special consideration, so that hilarity at late hours would not be disturbing to the family sleeping apartments. (Okie 1932, 7)

Finally, a section titled "Miscellaneous Notes" includes Okie's recording of the Behrends' preferences and concerns for a variety of issues, including the following:

- details on electrical systems including outlets, lightbulbs, fuses, and call buttons
- an "intercommunicating" telephone system with "long distance branches in Mr. Behrend's bedroom, sanctum, and elsewhere"
- bathrooms with the Behrends' specific brand requirements: standard plumbing, Chapman shower heads, Savoy toilets, and church saddle seats
- the use of fuel oil in addition to electric and coal as fuel (It was "doubtful that natural gas will be brought in. . . . Mr. Behrend is specifically interested in the Carrier system and wants full data.")

- the placement of the garage (If it was to be placed away from the house, could a place be found near the house where "one car could be run under cover at night"?)

With these guidelines and details agreed on, the architect and his clients were ready to proceed with the creation of an estate.

SUMMARY OF CONSTRUCTION

Although the details of construction as revealed in the correspondence are largely devoted to just a few buildings—primarily the house, its two additions, the bathhouse, and the chapel—several other buildings were constructed and existing buildings were renovated, often with several structures in progress at the same time. What follows is a list of the buildings for which Okie prepared sketches and blueprints and were constructed or added to as part of the Behrend estate. The accompanying "site plan," or map of the property, indicates the locations of the buildings. The following chapter considers the construction of the residence in greater detail, while chapter 4 reveals specifics related to the chapel and the outbuildings.

- The house on the hill. The main residence, referred to by the Behrends as the "House on the Hill," was never built. Okie devoted much effort to a host of sketches, models, and blueprints. However, the financial pressures of the Great Depression and a heartfelt affinity for the original "cottage" version of Glenhill led Mr. and Mrs. Behrend to revise and expand "Glen Cottage" and rename it "Glenhill Farmhouse" rather than build a much larger main residence as originally planned.
- Glenhill Farmhouse. The main house, known today as the Glenhill Farmhouse, had an evolving series of names in the correspondence between the Behrends and their architect. Originally referred to as the "Schilling House," the "cottage," or the "farmer's house," it later came to be referred to as "Glen Cottage" by Mrs. Behrend and finally as Glenhill. The house was built on the site of the house that had been owned by the Schilling family—the largest of the properties that the Behrends purchased in assembling their Glenhill

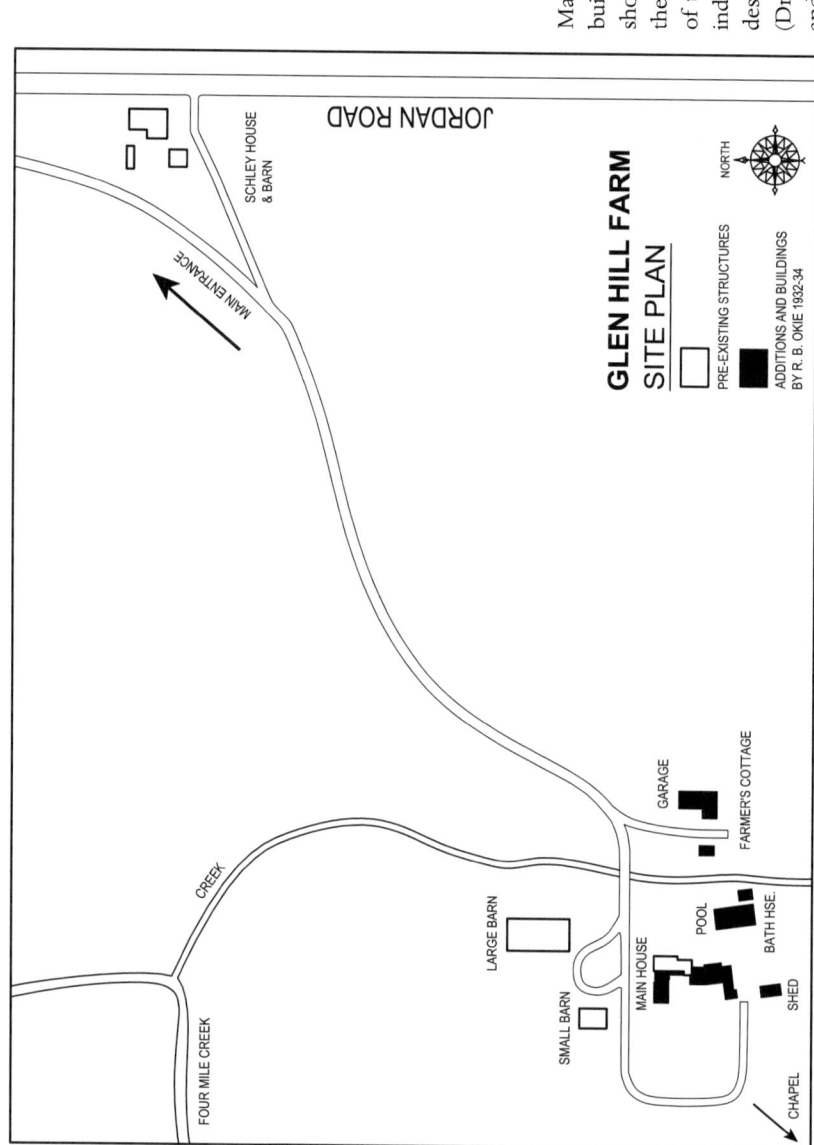

Map of Glenhill Farm buildings. This site plan shows the locations of the various buildings of the Glenhill estate, indicating those that Okie designed or modified. (Drawing by the author and James B. Garrison.)

GLEN HILL FARM
SITE PLAN

PRE-EXISTING STRUCTURES

ADDITIONS AND BUILDINGS
BY R. B. OKIE 1932-34

NORTH

JORDAN ROAD

SCHLEY HOUSE
& BARN

MAIN ENTRANCE

CREEK

FOUR MILE CREEK

LARGE BARN

SMALL BARN

MAIN HOUSE

GARAGE

FARMER'S COTTAGE

POOL

BATH HSE.

SHED

CHAPEL

acreage. Although it has been referred to as a "remodeling" (Lane 1998, 23) it is more properly regarded as new construction, since little of the original building was utilized.

The various names used for the house reflect both the evolving purpose and the size of the structure. Originally, this house was intended to serve as the quarters for the man in charge of the care of the estate and his family. He is referred to in the correspondence as the "farmer" or "superintendent," a position held at the time by Roy Bliley. The Behrends originally intended to live in this house only until their main residence—the house on the hill—could be built. Construction took place during the summer of 1932, with occupancy by the Behrends in November. Later, when the decision was made that this would become the main residence, two substantial additions were constructed that included larger quarters for the family and a "service wing" for the staff.

- The Schley House. Another property that the Behrends purchased to form the estate had been owned by the Schley family. The house was located on Jordan Road several hundred yards east of the Schilling residence. Under the original plan, it was to be converted for use as a "guesthouse." When the plans changed, it became the house for the farmer, Bliley, and his family. It was the first project completed on the estate, with occupancy by early fall 1932. The Schley garage or barn was also modified by Okie; however, the exact nature of the alterations to the house and barn are not certain, and photographic evidence is minimal. Decades later, after the property became part of Penn State, these buildings were sold and moved to another location on Jordan Road (Lane 1998, 50).
- Garage. The garage was constructed in late 1934. Built in an *L* shape, it was designed to provide space for five motor vehicles down the longer side and two small apartments for chauffeurs or other staff in the other wing.
- Shed. Also referred to as the "shelter shed," this Okie building was located south of the "service wing" addition to the house. It was accessed from the driveway and provided cover for up to three cars. It was built in 1934 but modified the following year.

- Bathhouse. Designed to resemble a colonial springhouse and built adjacent to the pool in 1934, the bathhouse provided changing rooms for those using the pool.
- Barns. Two barns, part of the Schilling property and located close to the house, were retained as part of the estate and core of central buildings. The "small barn" was altered by Okie, while the "large barn" appears not to have been changed by the architect.
- Chapel. The chapel was constructed in 1933 in the Wintergreen Gorge Cemetery. Not visible from the other buildings, it is about two-thirds of a mile away on the west side of Four Mile Creek, which winds northward toward Lake Erie, separating the estate from the cemetery.
- Farmer's office. Two wings were added to a small existing building to provide an office for the farmer and parking for two vehicles.
- Other construction. At least two other Glenhill estate features should be mentioned (neither are shown on the site plan). One is a "small cottage near Station Road" and its accompanying barn. No longer in existence, they are known to have been altered by Okie. Other remnants of the estate, located in the same vicinity, are the fieldstone pillars that to this day mark the driveway entrance to the property. They may be Okie designs. If not his design, then certainly they draw inspiration from the overall fieldstone motif. Okie created several plans for a gatehouse at that location near the driveway entrance. Never built, it may be that the two stone pillars are the much more modest result of a desire to mark the entry to the estate.

NOTE

1 The Ephrata Cloister, in Ephrata, Pennsylvania, housed a religious order in the early to mid-1700s. Noted for its historic architecture and art, it is maintained today as a state historic site by the Pennsylvania Historical and Museum Commission.

CHAPTER THREE

Building the Residence

By the spring of 1932, the Behrends were in a hurry to get started with construction. The strategy at this time was to build the "farmer's house," or "cottage," on the site of the Schilling residence. That was to be completed as quickly as possible so the Behrends could move to the estate from their longtime home at the paper plant. While the cottage was being built, they would work with Brognard Okie on plans for the main residence that they would occupy in a year or so. On May 2, Mr. Behrend's secretary, E. A. Ferguson, wrote to Okie, "As mentioned when you were here, Mr. and Mrs. Behrend are very anxious to get into the house on the farm as soon as possible" (Okie Papers). This is a theme that is repeated in the correspondence over coming months and years: please expedite the process.

In her very first letter to Okie, dated May 5, 1932, Mrs. Behrend talks about the receipt of the blueprints for the cottage and a decision that they have reached regarding housing for the maids. She writes,

Dear Mr. Okie—

Plans received today. It's all worked out nicely. We've spent time going over it and have decided to put the maids in a portable house in the orchard—well screened by trees and bushes—later to be removed at such time as we move up on the hill and the farmer moves in the cottage. (Okie Papers)

The Behrends never did "move up on the hill." Similarly, the maids were never put in temporary housing in the orchard—but these serve as prime examples of how uncertain and changeable the planning process was.

HOUSE ON THE HILL

The Behrends considered numerous plans for the house on the hill, and it is interesting to consider that aspect of the building and planning process. Okie's files reveal that he prepared drawings for six different versions of a main residence. Five of these were also made into three-dimensional models. Like many of his drawings in the file, the elevations are undated, but in the fall of 1932, as construction was nearing completion on the "farmer's house," the conversation again turned to what was planned to be the Behrends' main residence—the house on the hill, or sometimes just "Hill House." On September 9, 1932, in a multitopic letter, Okie wrote the following, addressed to Mr. Behrend, which indicated that plans and discussion were under way and alluded to an uncertainty of style:

> Within a few days we will send you two suggestions for the main house on the hill—one of a farm house type and the other a more formal house as we were discussing on Wednesday. (Okie Papers)

On September 29, in a letter to Okie, Mrs. Behrend acknowledged the receipt of two plans under consideration at that time. She also indicated her attraction to a Southern-style house that she had found in a magazine and sent a picture:

Model for the house on the hill. This is one of five models that Okie built of a main residence in 1932. While the models share a similar style, the layouts vary considerably. (Courtesy Pennsylvania State Archives.)

The two plans for the "Hill House" came. We are going off for a week and will take them along to look over.

Enclosed is a house I like in many ways. Are there any books of such Southern houses? These estates were dignified but also more or less informal and friendly. Should like to see how the other side of this house looks. (Okie Papers)

The reader wonders exactly what style of house Mrs. Behrend had found that she liked so well. There is no copy of the clipping she sent to Okie, yet this sounds like a change in direction—a turn away from the Pennsylvania farmhouse. In his next letter, Okie solved the mystery as to the type of house. He wrote on October 1,

Your letter of September 29th has just reached me. Also, the clipping of the Lee House, Stratford, in Virginia.

This is a beautiful old house and I will see if we have any photographs showing other views of it. The view that you have sent to me and which I return to you herewith is published in several of our architectural books. (Okie Papers)

Now referred to as "Stratford Hall" and serving as a museum, the estate in Northern Virginia was the birthplace of Robert E. Lee and dates to the early 1700s. The brick house is in the Georgian style (StratfordHall.org 2015). Looking back, it is somewhat surprising to find that the Behrends were considering a house in this style. However, Okie certainly would have been capable of designing such a home for the Behrends because he had worked in a variety of colonial styles over the course of his career, and one of his most important later works, Pennsbury Manor, is in a pre-Georgian style. Five of the six designs for the house on the hill are various forms of the Pennsylvania-farmhouse style. They do not look dissimilar from the end result that came with the additions to the farmer's cottage. However, the sixth elevation is a Georgian design in fieldstone and is probably a result of Mrs. Behrend's expression of interest in the appearance of Stratford Hall.

As 1932 drew to a close, so did construction on the "cottage" phase of the residence. By the middle of November, Glenhill was ready for its

Stratford Hall. This photograph from the Historic American Buildings Survey collection of the Library of Congress would have been similar to the picture that Mrs. Behrend sent to Okie, suggesting it might serve as a model for the house on the hill. (Courtesy Library of Congress.)

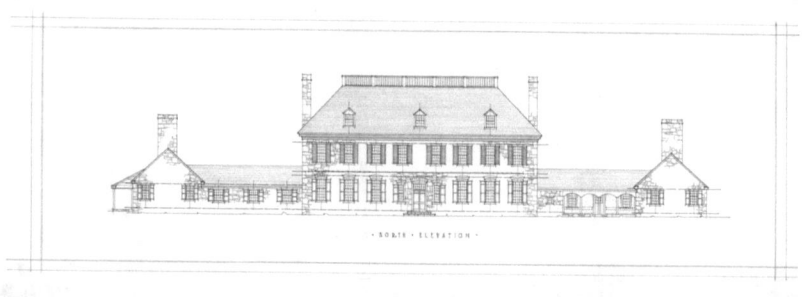

House on the hill, Georgian style. This proposed design for the Glenhill residence was likely a result of Mrs. Behrend's admiration for Stratford Hall and represented a distinct departure from the "Pennsylvania farm tradition" for which Okie was best known. (Courtesy Pennsylvania State Archives.)

owners, and the Behrends stayed for the first time in the house during Thanksgiving week with their daughter, who was home from college. A letter to Okie reveals Mr. Behrend's sense of humor and the family's satisfaction with the house:

> Harriet came home over Thanksgiving and last night we slept for the first time in your house. Everything was O.K(ie). We like the house very much. (November 25, 1932, Okie Papers)

The conversation between architect and client regarding changes to the cottage and plans for the house on the hill continued into early 1933. Okie wrote several detailed letters. In one, he proposed adding servants' quarters to the cottage rather than constructing a separate house for the staff on the west side of the house (Okie to Mrs. Behrend, January 9, 1933, Okie Papers). On January 28, Okie proposed the following solution to the question of the house on the hill:

> In thinking over the question of your work at the farm near Erie, it seems to me it would be advisable to build on the site of the proposed larger house on the hill a decidedly smaller building that would be appropriate for Mrs. Behrend and you. This would give you an opportunity to enjoy the site on the hill that you like so much and at the same time have the quiet and seclusion that you will not be able to get at the little farm house. (Okie to Mr. Behrend, Okie Papers)

The "site on the hill that you like so much" might have provided a view of Lake Erie in the distance. The location was most likely a short distance from the Glenhill residence where the land rises up a hill on the south side. However, it was not to be. Mr. Behrend responds immediately to Okie from the Arrowhead Springs Hotel in California. He and Mrs. Behrend were dividing their time in February and March between the Arrowhead Springs Hotel and the Arizona Biltmore in Phoenix. Although still leaving open the possibility of the house on the hill, this letter in early February seems to be the turning point in the Behrends' thinking on the matter, after

Farmer's cottage completed. This photograph shows the completed farmer's cottage during the winter of 1932–33. The decision to put two large additions on it had not yet been made. (Courtesy Penn State Behrend Archives.)

Aerial view, winter 1932–33. The driveway cuts through the center of this southward-looking photograph. Above the driveway (left to right) are the swimming pool, the farmer's cottage version of Glenhill, and the tennis court. Below the driveway are the large barn and the unaltered small barn. (Courtesy Penn State Behrend Archives.)

which they turn their attention toward making additions to the cottage and abandon talk of the house on the hill:

Dear Mr. Okie,

Your letter of Jan. 28 has been rec'd via Erie. . . . It was nice to hear from you. House on the Hill. Business is in such a condition, we had to lay off so many people, demands on me for help are constantly increasing while my income decreases, that we can't even flirt with that idea at the present time. Please do nothing about it therefore, until we can tell you to proceed. Let us hope that we may soon be able to do so. (Mr. Behrend to Okie, February 3, 1933, Okie Papers)

It is apparent that finances were a key reason to put off construction of the house on the hill. At the date of this letter from Mr. Behrend in early 1933, the Great Depression was in full swing and unemployment was high, and Hammermill Paper's business had hit a low point. Clearly the idea of building the main residence had lost its luster. During their two-month vacation out West, the Behrends' thinking shifted to the concept of adding two additions to their completed cottage. No longer would the cottage be intended for the farmer and his family; rather, it would be their home.

In early March, Mrs. Behrend wrote to Okie from California. She made specific suggestions to previous plans—not for a house on the hill but for additions to the cottage—and she included not only a drawing but also a model that she had constructed:

Mr. Behrend has had the Flu, and while he was ill I amused myself with plans. With banks closing and everything so uncertain we may not build any more, but here are some ideas. Probably they won't work out to scale but it seemed to me we could get about all we need with one wing instead of two. (March 2, 1933, Okie Papers)

Mrs. Behrend went on to make a series of suggestions, and a week later, Okie sent a reply:

ARROWHEAD
SPRINGS ▼ HOTEL

THE HOTTEST CURATIVE SPRINGS KNOWN

H. S. WARD
MANAGING DIRECTOR

ARROWHEAD SPRINGS
CALIFORNIA

Febr. 3ᵈ 1933.

Dear Mr. Okie,

You letter of Jan. 28. has
just been rec'd via Erie. I am
sending my reply to Mr. Ferguson,
so that he may retain a copy.
It was nice to hear from you.
House on the Hill. Business is
in such a condition, we had to
lay off so many people, demands
on me for help are constantly
increasing while my income
decreases, that we can't even
flirt with that idea at the
present time. Please do nothing
about it therefore, until we
can tell you to proceed. Let us
hope that we may soon
be able to do so.

Letter from the Arrowhead Springs Hotel. This letter (page one of two) is unusual in that it is one of only a few handwritten letters from Mr. Behrend to Okie. (Courtesy Pennsylvania State Archives.)

Mr. and Mrs. Behrend on horseback in the desert. Although undated, this photograph was likely taken while the Behrends were staying at the Arizona Biltmore in the winter of 1933. (Courtesy Penn State Behrend Archives.)

Your letter of March 2ⁿᵈ reached me a day or two ago and I was very sorry to hear that Mr. Behrend had had an attack of the Flu. I hope by this time he is entirely recovered. . . . The model was pretty well smashed up when it arrived but we are plastering it together and will try to work out a rough plan of the first and second floors in accordance with your sketches and the model. (March 10, 1933, Okie Papers)

Ultimately, two substantial additions were added to the cottage. One addition—on the south side and extending to the west—served as the "service wing" and included the kitchen, laundry, and five bedrooms for the servants or staff. The second addition was on the north side of the house

Enlarging Glenhill
Farm house---adding
bedrooms, living
room, new kitchen,
etc. - 1934

Building an addition. By early 1934, the "service wing" was being constructed on the south side of the house. This photograph and the original caption beneath it are likely the handiwork of Mrs. Behrend. (Courtesy Penn State Behrend Archives.)

and also extended to the west; it provided living space for the family on the lower level with bedrooms on the second floor. Construction on the additions (first the service wing and later the family wing) was under way by early 1934 and completed by the end of that year.

GLENHILL RESIDENCE: FEATURES AND DESIGN

One of Okie's trademark features was his concern with how the house and other buildings were arranged in relation to the site and to each other. His thinking on this topic is elaborated in the introduction that he wrote for Eleanor Raymond's book of photographs of colonial Pennsylvania buildings:

> As we travel through the country we are impressed with the good judgment and the artistic sense which those who first located the houses and the various out-buildings used in selecting sites for them. It is remarkable how cleverly they located the house itself and each of the buildings around the house, and the relation of one to the other. . . . One of the chief charms of these old buildings is the natural way in which they fit the ground. Whether on the side of a hill with entrance doors at both upper and lower levels, or with practically flat ground around the house the effect is invariably restful and inviting. (Okie [1931] 1977)

In an early letter regarding one of several plans that he had prepared for the main residence, Okie revealed how he placed importance on the siting of Glenhill:

> The house, as we have suggested it, fits the grades pretty nicely, putting steps in several locations with the floor levels suiting as nearly as it can be arranged the existing outside grades. . . . I think the arrangement of the swimming pool, access from the pool to Mr. Behrend's quarters with little narrow steps, the large fireplace at the side of the pool, etc., all will give a very convenient arrangement and one that will look very natural in the location. (Okie to Spencer Gordon, February 11, 1932, Okie Papers)

The residence and other buildings that made up Glenhill Farm were of fieldstone construction—another trademark of Okie's designs. The random pattern of the stone is referred to as "rubble" and follows the tradition of the earliest stone houses in the Delaware Valley, which "were built of local stone recovered from farm fields after being brought to the surface by plowing . . . the individual pieces had weathered faces and were of random size and shape" (Richie, Milner, and Huber 2005, 18). Another Okie trademark is the fieldstone chimneys, with which Glenhill is well endowed: "Chimneys are a feature of his houses, just as are the fireplaces within. Of generous size, beautifully proportioned, they are always well related to walls and roofs" (Koyl 1949).

Although a traditional feature of colonial architecture is the use of local materials, the correspondence reveals that a number of Glenhill's materials came from afar. An example of this is the "Avondale" stone for at least some of the fireplace hearths for Glenhill, which came from Southeastern Pennsylvania. Okie wrote to Spencer Gordon, mentioning DeYenno, the mason from Devon, near Philadelphia:

> Regarding the stone for the hearths at Mr. Behrend's I have just seen Mr. DeYenno who tells me the Pennsylvania Railroad have given him a price of $.53 per cwt. for shipping the stone by freight. I felt this was reasonable and have asked Mr. DeYenno to go right ahead with the order.
>
> The stone will be shipped from Devon and Mr. DeYenno will give me the car number and other information that you require which I will send you as soon as I receive it from him. He proposes to ship about a ton of stone and they will all be lettered on the back. (July 6, 1932, Okie Papers)

As with the stone for the hearths, Okie was very much concerned about the use of other high-quality materials. Sometimes this took the form of antique materials, and the letters reveal that Okie searched for antique hardware, lamps, sconces, and doors. This led him to contact various antique dealers or to visit old houses. For instance, he wrote to Mrs. Behrend about his search for colonial-era paneling for the residence in a historic section of Philadelphia:

> I am going with a contractor this afternoon to see an old house in Germantown that he is taking down and in which he says there is some attractive

panelling, also some mantles in which we might be interested. (June 20, 1932, Okie Papers)

Not all of these searches were successful, and the following day, Okie reported back to Mrs. Behrend:

> I find there is practically nothing in this building that would be of inter-est to you except some old glass and a very small amount of hardware. The house was of a rather late period with pretty high ceilings and the interior woodwork was, in my judgement, not worth shipping to Erie. (Okie Papers)

Nevertheless, these anecdotes convey the amount of effort and commit-ment that Okie gave to the work and the extent to which he tried to incor-porate actual colonial-era materials into his buildings.

The exterior design of Glenhill, like other Okie designs, is meant to serve several purposes. As has been noted, the "additive" nature suggests that it was built over the course of many years as the homeowner was able to afford to expand the house. The design is also intended not only to be attractive and interesting but to appear small in scale. The author Margaret Richie, in describing another Okie property—Peaceable Farm in Bucks County—identifies architectural features that describe Glenhill as well: "As was customary with Okie houses, the exterior massing is broken down into components of varying heights. The result is a building with different roof-lines, perpendicular wings, and façade set-backs, creating a composition of considerable aesthetic interest and an intimate scale" (Richie, Milner, and Huber 2005, 39). Glenhill, when viewed from any angle, does not appear to be a large house, belying its total size of more than 8,200 square feet.

Another unique feature of Glenhill and an Okie trademark is the use of "wall dormers." Unlike traditional dormers that sit higher on the roof, the wall dormers "break through the roof eaves to form a serrated pro-file, as well as interesting arrangements of gutters and downspouts to animate the walls." They were uncommon in American architecture but could be found in European buildings (Garrison 2013, 18). It is clear that

Glenhill exterior features. From the southeast corner, some of Okie's distinguishing features that are evident include the facade setbacks, box cornices, shed roof at the entryways, low stone walls for the walkways, and three-stone lintels above some of the windows. (Photograph by the author.)

Swimming pool. Taken near the bathhouse, this is one of the photographs of noted residential photographer Harold Haliday Costain of Scarsdale, New York, whom the Behrends hired to photograph the house in 1936. It shows the east side of Glenhill. (Courtesy Penn State Behrend Archives.)

North facade. Another Costain photograph, this view of the north side was taken near the small barn. The stone portion to the left represents the original "farmer's cottage," while the clapboard and stone sections to the right represent the addition of the family wing. (Courtesy Penn State Behrend Archives.)

North facade today. Okie trademarks include the rubble-pattern stonework, a wall dormer (upper right window) with accompanying wall-mounted box gutter, and the white "biscuit-top" fence on a stone wall. (Photograph by the author.)

Window, east side. This small window possesses a three-stone lintel with a center keystone. Adjacent is an antique reproduction lamp. (Photograph by the author.)

Living room. The living room and its alcoves include ornamental woodwork, Palladian arches, and Doric pilasters. A portrait of Mrs. Behrend hangs above the fireplace. (Photograph by RFrank Photography.)

Alcove storage. The living room alcoves include small cabinets with hand-crafted antique reproduction hinges and a small drawer. These are typical of numerous storage spaces throughout the house. (Photograph by the author.)

Antique hardware. This hinge is typical of the antique or antique-reproduction hardware that is found throughout the Glenhill buildings. The firm of I. Marshall of Philadelphia was awarded the contract for the residence, while Myron Teller of Kingston, New York, produced the handmade wrought-iron hardware for the chapel. (Photograph by the author.)

Door detail. (Photograph by RFrank Photography.)

Library fireplace. Okie's plans called for "Avondale" stone for the hearths in the cottage version of Glenhill, shipped from Devon on the Pennsylvania Railroad. (Photograph by RFrank Photography.)

Mr. Behrend's bedroom. This is from the series of photographs by Harold Haliday Costain. (Courtesy Penn State Behrend Archives.)

Dining room. This is another Costain photograph. (Courtesy Penn State Behrend Archives.)

Guest bedroom. This Costain photograph shows the fireplace and woodwork found in the first-floor guest bedroom. (Courtesy Penn State Behrend Archives.)

Mrs. Behrend appreciated this aspect of the design as she wrote to Okie as construction proceeded:

> The cottage is more interesting all the time. I like the rain conductors between the dormers—and other details. Are leaving Monday for Michigan for ten days or so. Trust the house will be ready for us . . . upon our return. (July 22, 1932, Okie Papers)

Other Okie architectural features that can be found at Glenhill are shown in the accompanying photographs. These include the use of antique or antique-reproduction hardware, both inside and out, especially the hinges for the doors and windows. The box cornice is another Okie detail—this is the exterior carpentry feature found at the intersection of the roof and the wall, visible on the residence, chapel, and bathhouse. Three-stone lintels are found above many of the Glenhill windows, with the middle stone in a keystone shape; other windows have an arched segmental lintel. Additional exterior details include the "shed" roof at the entries; the wooden "biscuit-top" fence painted white, found on top of a low stone wall; and the varied rooflines and facade setbacks, expressing the additive quality.

A widely used interior feature in Glenhill is the presence of built-in furniture, such as bookcases and china closets. This was not unique to Glenhill or to Okie's homes, but it was common to much colonial revival architecture and was especially prevalent in living rooms and dining rooms (May 1991, 119). Other interior features include the use of colonial paneling and other woodwork of high quality, including ornamental woodwork; the extensive use of casework with numerous nooks for storage; and low ceilings. Commenting on one of these features, Mrs. Behrend wrote,

> The cottage (Glen Cottage) is almost done. It surely is full of funny little cupboards and what all—to which Mr. Sessinghaus and I added towel racks and shelves of wood. (Mrs. Behrend to Okie, September 29, 1932, Okie Papers)

Ernst Behrend's letters in 1932 reflect an interest in the architectural issues related to technology, including securing excellent materials and maintaining the conveniences to which he was accustomed. What follows is a sampling from several of his typically brief letters in May, when he was quite active in making requests and posing questions to Okie—in this case, recommending the shower seat from his new yacht and asking about a brand of insulation:

> Enclosed is sketch of a shower bath seat which I have aboard the *Amida*. It is very handy.
>
> Does the attached pamphlet from the Celotex Company have any interest for us? (May 20, 1932, Okie Papers)

The next day, Mr. Behrend wrote to ask Okie whether lightning rods should be installed on the house. That question resulted in a detailed response from the architect, which is interesting in part because it makes reference to two unique features of his house—large chimneys and the use of cypress shingles imported from Louisiana. Okie wrote,

In reply to your letter of May 21st regarding the danger from fire at the farm house, I do not know whether lightning rods are of any real use. A good many people have faith in them and they have been put on quite a number of the buildings that we have completed. . . . With the split cypress shingle roof and the chimneys carried quite a distance above the roof, as they will be, I do not think there is any particular danger from sparks, at least, until the shingles have gotten quite old and soft. (May 24, 1932, Okie Papers)

Okie replied to each of Mr. Behrend's various questions and recommendations, be they about the plumbing and heating systems, bathroom fixtures, insulation, fireplaces, bathtubs, and more. A letter from Mr. Behrend to Okie a few weeks later is particularly interesting:

Many thanks for your promptness in sending us the plumbing specifications. They were at the hotel for us on our arrival last evening. It was very helpful to have them when we called at the Kohler Company to-day.

Gov. Kohler is a friend of ours and we like to try his fittings! (June 8, 1932, Okie Papers)

Mr. Behrend was referring to Walter J. Kohler Sr., who had served as the governor of Wisconsin from 1929 to 1931 and was the president of the Kohler Company, known for the production of plumbing equipment and other goods, located in Kohler, Wisconsin (Karges 2000). It is not known how the Behrends came to make his acquaintance, but clearly they considered him among their friends and wanted to send some business his way.

During the summer of 1933, the Behrends enjoyed the cottage while waiting to finalize plans for the additions, but Mr. Behrend had a matter that concerned him:

Dear Mr. Okie:

Our stay in the country, within and without your house, is very pleasant, and we shall be sorry to move into town during the winter. There are some drawbacks which, in the course of time, we hope to overcome.

One of these drawbacks is that the great pleasure of taking meals out of doors is now contested by the flies. Have you a solution? We thought today that you might design a screened eating pavilion near the swimming pool, detracting as little as possible from the outdoors aspect. It should be large enough to accommodate from sixteen to twenty people. Could you send us a little sketch showing this idea? Of course, whatever we do, we should do immediately.

We also thought that in the meantime we might put an overhead slowly-turning fan with long blades on a temporary framework over the table, but this, I fear will only be partly effective. (July 19, 1933, Okie Papers)

Interestingly, Mr. Behrend's engineering instincts proved to be correct, as a subsequent letter revealed that a fan did indeed solve the problem of meals being "contested by the flies."

A strong reliance on magazine articles and books on colonial architecture is found throughout the correspondence. Working on plans for the additions in late 1933, Mrs. Behrend found guidance in a book that Okie had loaned them in regard to the style of the interior woodwork and design of the living room. Titled *Homes of Our Ancestors*, it shows what is referred to as the "Woodbury Long Island Room." This room is from a colonial house that had been reassembled and made into a permanent display at New York's Metropolitan Museum of Art (Halsey and Tower 1925, plate 7). Mrs. Behrend suggested that they copy the room:

> It is a question whether we would like this room copied directly from the room in the Metropolitan Museum which is called the "Woodbury Long Island Room." . . . As complete drawings come for this . . . why would it not be best to copy them exactly? (December 17, 1933, Okie Papers)

Although not an exact copy, Okie's designs for both the living room and the dining room of Glenhill possess strong similarities to the Woodbury Long Island room in terms of the woodwork, making use of colonial-era designs such as Doric pilasters and Palladian arches. (The room remains on display at the museum but is now referred to as the John Hewlett house.)

One of the last parts of the construction involved the flooring. The correspondence reveals the persistence that was involved in Okie's work as he engaged Harold Hipple the contractor and mill owner in Harrisburg to search for antique lumber. References to Hipple's search for flooring for the family addition to the Glenhill residence are found in several letters. Starting his search in December 1933, after several failures and about to give up, Hipple finally found what he was looking for "back of Williamsport" the following summer. What they were seeking was "cork pine"— that is, pine from mature white pine trees no longer readily available. He planned to transport the lumber to Harrisburg, where he would plane it for flooring. These passages from three of Hipple's letters give the details:

I have run down four or five prospects from my advertisements but the quality was not good. I heard of a very old lumber settlement back of Williamsport. . . . I am leaving to-morrow to inspect it. If this proves a failure I will have to give it up. (Hipple to Okie, June 29, 1934, Okie Papers)

On July 2, Hipple found what they wanted:

My brother and I was fortunate to find some of the original Penna. cork pine, which I think is just what you have been looking for for some time. . . . I am expressing samples, and have picked out what I call the worst conditions. . . . This lumber is about one hours drive back of Williamsport and with bad roads it takes considerable time to get it to Harrisburg to work. If it is satisfactory do not delay in approving the samples. (Okie Papers)

With Okie's approval, delivery was made:

The trucks arrived at 2 o'clock this morning with the lumber and they were loaded with the most beautiful white pine I ever seen. . . . You would have thought I was taking gold out of the man's pocket when the two trucks drove away with this lumber, as he thought he owned a gold mine instead of lumber and would not permit any of it to be loaded until the cash was handed over to him. (July 10, 1934, Okie Papers)

With the exception of the living room, construction was sufficiently completed by August so that the family could move into the renovated residence. The Behrends certainly appeared to be satisfied with the final product, as Mrs. Behrend wrote to Okie some months later,

We find our house very comfortable and pleasant, and everyone coming here seems greatly pleased with it. (January 14, 1935, Okie Papers)

In a letter in which he sent Okie a final payment for the additions to the house, Mr. Behrend wrote,

It has been a great pleasure to work with you and your brother, and your house is admired by all who come to see it. (June 11, 1935, Okie Papers)

With the completion of the Glenhill Farmhouse and its two large additions, the question arises as to the degree to which the completed residence contained the features that had been intended in the original concept of the house on the hill. Did the Behrends ultimately obtain the house that they wanted? In fact, by closely comparing the features that Okie had outlined and described in his detailed memorandum to the final floor plans of the completed house, the evidence strongly suggests that virtually all the elements were incorporated. The first floor of the completed house had a living room measuring twenty feet by thirty feet as originally stipulated (although it was not designed as a library as specified in the original memorandum); an office for Mr. Behrend; an "ample" dining room; a breakfast room, or "dining alcove"; a reception room; and a guest room with private bath. In addition, it had a good-sized library but appears to have lacked "a hybrid sunroom and porch." The second-floor family wing contained the three family suites for Mr. Behrend, Mrs. Behrend, and Miss Behrend, each with a bath, a dressing room, plenty of closets and wardrobe space, access to a sun porch, and for Mr. Behrend, a "sleeping porch." There were two guest rooms with private baths. The ground floor of the service wing contained a kitchen, pantry, laundry room, cook's pantry, butler's room and bath, and a second servant's bedroom ("boy's bedroom") with a private bath. On the second floor were three bedrooms for servants with a shared bath and a large linen closet.

Living room detail. "The most beautiful white pine I ever seen," declared Harold Hipple regarding the lumber intended for the flooring in the family addition. (Photograph by RFrank Photography.)

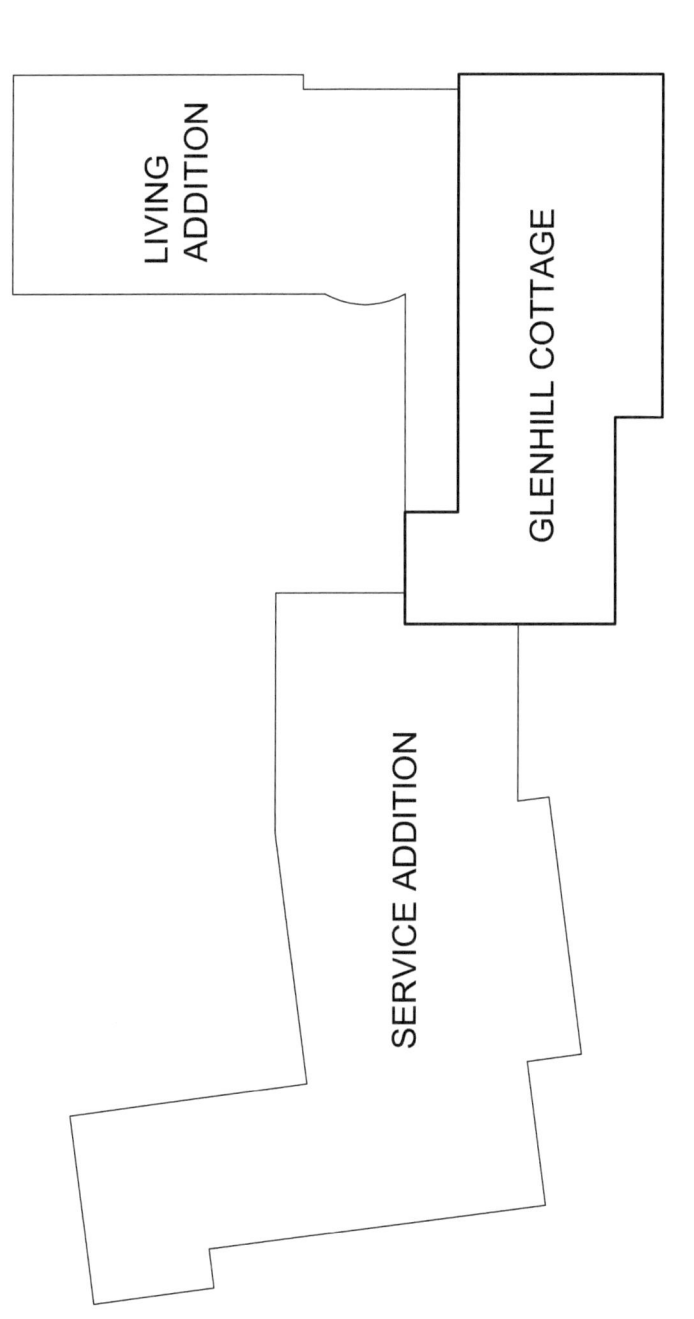

LIVING ADDITION

GLENHILL COTTAGE

SERVICE ADDITION

BUILDING OUTLINE

House with additions. This drawing shows the outline of the original "Glenhill Cottage," completed in November 1932, and the two additions built in 1934. (Drawing by James B. Garrison.)

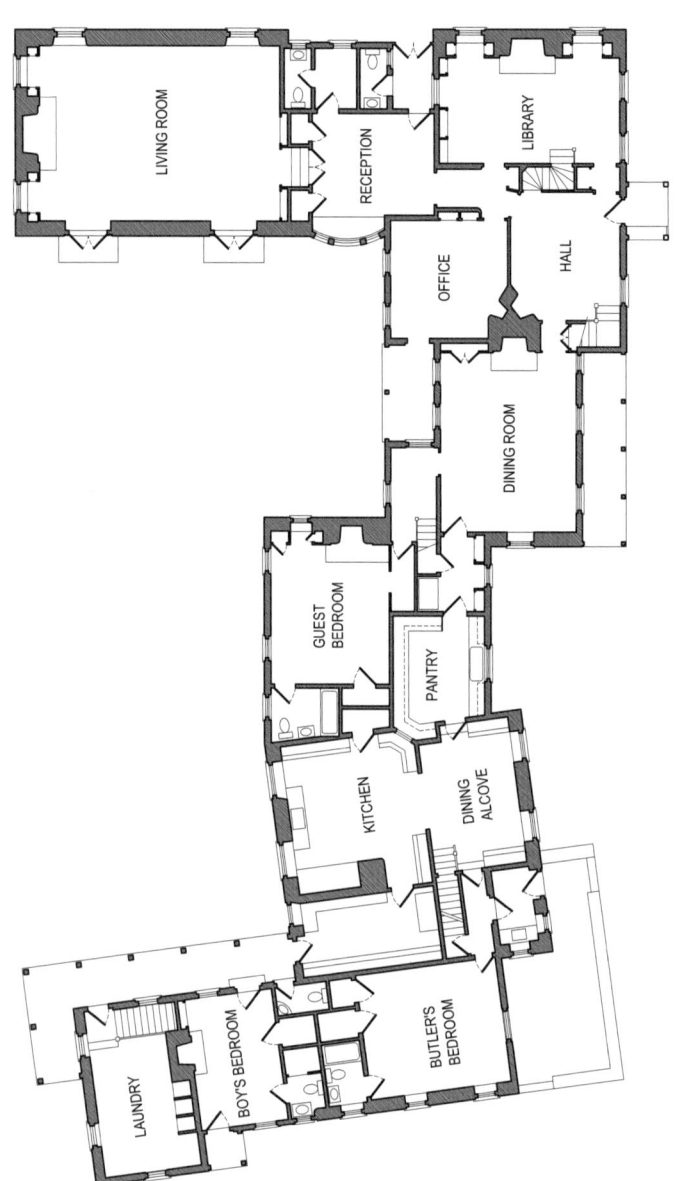

FIRST FLOOR PLAN

0   5   10   20 FEET

First-floor plan. This is a rendering of Okie's final floor plan for the first floor of Glenhill. (Drawing by James B. Garrison.)

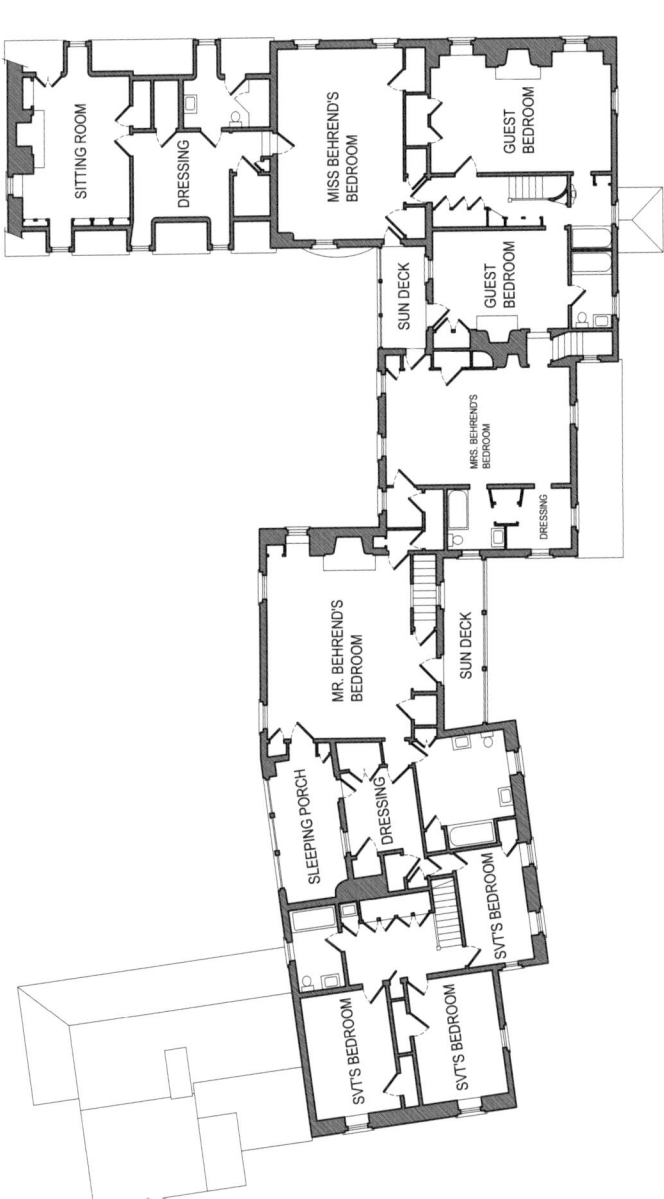

SECOND FLOOR PLAN

0   5   10   20 FEET

Second-floor plan. Like the first-floor plan, this is dated February 1934 and shows the plan for what became the final version of Glenhill. (Drawing by James B. Garrison.)

In all, the house had eleven bedrooms, twelve bathrooms or lavatories, and thirteen fireplaces. Renovations to the small barn are thought to have provided the "recreation area" that Okie had described in his original memorandum for use by Harriet and her friends. Features mentioned in the memorandum that were lacking in the finished house were a large staircase with a landing large enough for a writing desk, a sewing room in the service wing, an elevator, and a sitting room with a fireplace as part of Mrs. Behrend's bedroom suite. Relative to the overall size of the residence, these seem like fairly modest sacrifices. For the most part, the final version of Glenhill contained the priorities outlined for the house on the hill, although it lacked a view of Lake Erie, which had been under consideration in the early planning for the large house.

CHAPTER FOUR

Construction of the Outbuildings and Chapel

In addition to the Glenhill Farmhouse, a series of other buildings were designed or modified by Brognard Okie. They are represented to considerably varying degrees in the documents in the state archives. The chapel—for reasons that will be revealed—was the center of much correspondence. On the other hand, very little was recorded about the garage, the farmer's office, or the other existing buildings to which modifications are known to have been made. This chapter addresses some of what the Behrend-Okie correspondence has to say about these buildings.

BATHHOUSE

A common sight on a colonial farm in Southeastern Pennsylvania was the springhouse. Used to refrigerate milk and other food, the stone structure was built directly over a spring, making use of the continual supply of cold water (Lanier and Herman 1997, 55). It was Okie's idea that a "dressing room or small living room" be constructed next to the swimming pool at Glenhill. The building would imitate the springhouse of old, thereby contributing to the desired effect of the early Pennsylvania farm tradition while providing for the needs of those using the swimming pool. In the correspondence, the Behrends and Okie eventually came to refer to the building as the bathhouse.

Okie had referred the Behrends to Eleanor Raymond's 1931 book, which presents a photographic record of the farmhouses and outbuildings

PLATE 89

See Measured Drawing, Plate 111

SPRING HOUSE NEAR CHESTER SPRINGS, CHESTER COUNTY

PLATE 90

Springhouses, Chester County, Pennsylvania. These two spring-houses, as found in Eleanor Raymond's book on early Pennsylvania architecture, were admired by Mrs. Behrend. (Courtesy Schiffer.)

SMOKE AND SPRING HOUSE AT BUCKTOWN, CHESTER COUNTY

of the southeastern counties of colonial Pennsylvania. Mrs. Behrend liked the features of springhouses found in the book, and Okie made use of her preferences when he designed the building. Plates 89 and 90 from the book are reproduced in the accompanying photographs.

The bathhouse is actually built on a site that slopes down to a small creek that runs just to the east side of the house beyond the swimming pool. In his letter from August 22, 1932, Okie wrote the following in regard to his plans for the bathhouse, which would also include equipment related to the swimming pool:

> You will notice the lower floor of the building, which is only a slight distance above the level of the stream, provides for a small room to be as much like a spring house as possible, and adjoining this spring house a room for the filters and a heater room.
>
> The spring house is at the upper end which is deeper in the bank and would be the natural place for a spring—In fact, I am in hopes when the excavating is done for the building that you will strike a spring in this location.
>
> The upper level, which corresponds with the level of the walk around the pool, provides a little living room or sitting room with a fireplace, a room for a shower, a toilet and a little dressing room, with stone steps leading from the living room to the walk around the swimming pool.
>
> In drawing out these sketches we have tried to adapt the two plate numbers in Miss Raymond's book that Mrs. Behrend particularly liked—The outside steps leading to the high-up door, chimney, etc., as per plate #90, and the spring house roof and entrance somewhat like plate #89. (Okie to Mr. Behrend, Okie Papers)

In his introduction to Eleanor Raymond's book, Okie provided some insight into what he admired about the traditional domestic buildings of Southeastern Pennsylvania: "Those who built these old buildings, whether of stone, brick, logs, or frame, had certainly a keen sense of proportion. They knew exactly where to place their doors and windows, and how to design their cornices. . . . It is a fact that the old buildings existing today are beautifully proportioned, even the simplest woodshed or spring house

Bathhouse. Looking southwest, this photograph shows the north and east facades of the bathhouse. The land slopes down to a small creek on the east side, mimicking the logical placement of a colonial springhouse. (Photograph by the author.)

Bathhouse, west facade. The bathhouse provided changing rooms for those using the swimming pool. (Photograph by RFrank Photography.)

or bake oven having a charm of its own" (Okie [1931] 1977). Clearly Okie intended to endow the Glenhill buildings with these attributes, and there can be little doubt that the bathhouse at Glenhill Farm possesses a "charm of its own" as a modern version of a colonial springhouse.

Construction on the bathhouse was probably completed sporadically during the summer and fall of 1934, but the computation of Okie's fee presented a challenge. Normally the Behrends paid him within several months of completion of a building. His fee amounted to 10 percent of construction costs, and he relied on the Behrends to inform him of the total costs, since they paid the majority of the contractors directly. However, only a portion of the bathhouse had been built by the contractor, the Erie firm of Sessinghaus and Ostergaard, at a charge of $635.08, which probably included all the masonry. The remainder of the work was done by the Behrends' resident carpenter at the farm. On May 27, 1935, Mrs. Behrend explained to Okie how difficult it was for them to present him with a firm figure for the bathhouse:

> It would be difficult for us to figure just what the bath house cost us because stone was hauled, part of which was used in the bath house, part for walks, and part for the foundation. It would be almost impossible to segregate these items. It would also be difficult to figure how much was paid to our carpenter for the work he did on the bath house, because, as you know, he would work there part of the time and elsewhere at other times. (Okie Papers)

They agreed to settle the bill for the bathhouse at a later time.

SHELTER SHED

Referred to variously in the correspondence as the "shelter shed," the "shelter," or the "shed," this building's interior dimensions originally measured twenty-nine feet wide and fourteen feet deep. It was built close to the south side of the house for the purpose of providing cover for the automobiles when it was not convenient to park them in the more remote garage location. As Okie had written in his original memo describing the Behrends' priorities,

It is understood that if a garage is located some distance from the house, somewhere—possibly in connection with the service wing—a place might be found where one car could be run under cover at night. (Okie 1932, 10)

Indeed, the shelter shed is located only a few steps from the back door of the "service wing" addition to the house. However, its appearance today is misleading in regard to the original design, which was open to the elements on the west side.

The shelter shed, as revealed in the correspondence, was the cause of great dissatisfaction on the part of Mrs. Behrend and considerable regret on the part of Brognard Okie. While it was intended to shelter automobiles, it was not nearly deep enough to do that effectively. In spite of Okie's close attention to detail in nearly all matters, the dimensions of the shelter shed seem to have been an oversight on his part. The building was open to the west side, and although the roof extended several feet beyond the foundation, the interior dimension of fourteen feet would not have been nearly deep enough for the Behrends' Cadillac, the various models of which were typically between seventeen and twenty feet long at that time (Classic Caddys, n.d.). It was also too short for their other cars, including the 1929 Duesenberg—widely regarded as the most luxurious and expensive car on the American market. Open on the side of the prevailing westerly winds in a part of the country well known for its lake-effect snow, the shelter shed seems a poor design. In the fall of 1934, Mrs. Behrend wrote to Okie,

The shed for the cars is far too short. . . . I knew it would not take the Cadillac, but all cars seem to stick out and get rained on. (Okie Papers, September 30, 1934)

I do not feel we will do anything about it at this time as it would be quite an expensive proposition. . . . All our cars are much too long to be accommodated in the shelter, and right now we find it very hard on the cars to leave them out in the snow and rain. (November 17, 1934, Okie Papers)

Shelter shed today. The west side of the shelter shed, originally open to the elements and providing only marginal cover to the Behrends' automobiles, has since been enclosed and serves as a college office. The slight angle in the roof indicates the location where the building originally ended before Okie modified it to better accommodate the cars. (Photograph by the author.)

House and shelter shed. This early photograph shows the newly completed house from the west. Note that the shelter shed appears to the far right and, as originally designed, is open to the westerly winds. (Courtesy Penn State Behrend Archives.)

Over the following months, Mrs. Behrend considered several options, including adding a grape arbor to provide protection at the end of the shed or having the contractor, Sessinghaus and Ostergaard, lengthen it and add overhead doors, apparently without the benefit (or expense) of Okie's involvement. Okie was clearly concerned for a couple of reasons. On the one hand, he regretted the situation: "Mrs. Behrend is apparently very much dissatisfied with the depth of the shed and I regret this fact exceedingly." However, he was also concerned lest something be done to "spoil the looks of the Shelter" (Okie to Sessinghaus and Ostergaard, November 21, 1934, Okie Papers). It appears that a sort of compromise was reached, and the following summer, Okie-designed changes were made to the building, extending the roof on the west side and preserving an attractive appearance.

GARAGE AND THE FARMER'S OFFICE
Part of the core of Glenhill buildings, the garage and the farmer's office are located beyond the small creek on the east side of the residence. They are both accessed from a spur that shoots off from the main driveway. Neither

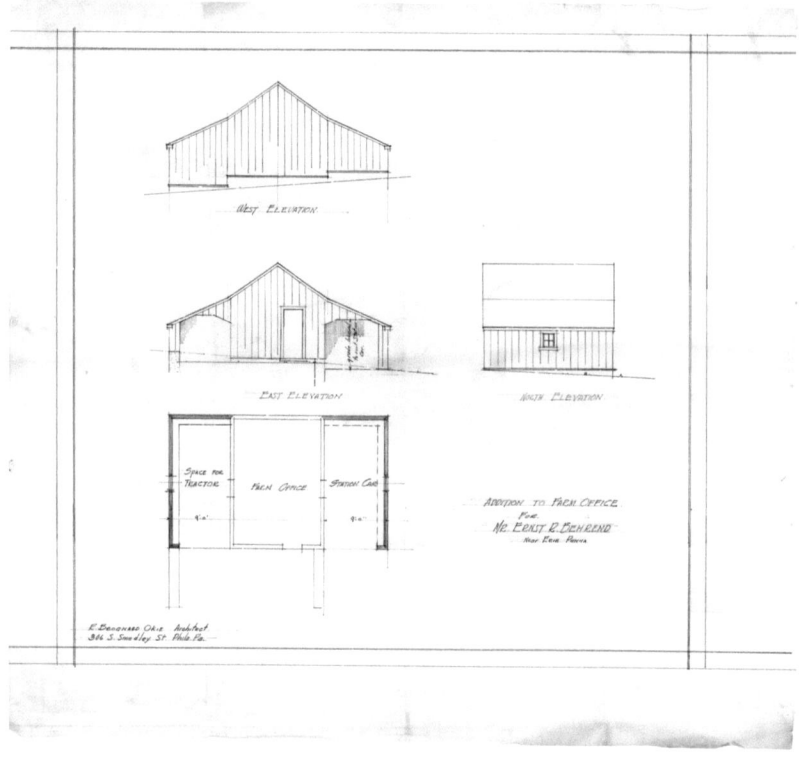

Drawings of the farmer's office. This series of drawings by Okie shows the modifications that he made to a small existing building to make it more useful and to give it a more traditional appearance. (Courtesy Pennsylvania State Archives.)

"Dear Mr. Okie—Where is the Hardware?" The farmer's office (or as Mrs. Behrend refers to it here, the farm garage) was among the first buildings to be worked on. In November 1932, she was anxious that the doors be put on the building: "They are worried for fear the south wind will damage building without doors. In haste M. B. Behrend." Since all the hardware was custom made according to Okie's specification, a trip to the hardware store was not an option. (Courtesy Pennsylvania State Archives.)

Farmer's office and bathhouse in winter. From the driveway, looking southwest, this early photograph shows the farmer's office (undergoing modifications) and, behind it, the bathhouse. (Courtesy Penn State Behrend Archives.)

building received any noteworthy discussion in the correspondence. For the farmer's office, Okie domesticated an existing small rectangular building by adding two wings to give it a traditional appearance. The wings were intended to provide storage space for the farm's tractor and the "station car," while the center of the building served as the farm manager's office.

The garage was a substantial building in an L shape and is the largest of the Okie-designed outbuildings at the core of the estate. One wing provided garage space for five vehicles, and the other wing provided living quarters for the two chauffeurs, one on the first floor and the other on the second floor. The correspondence reveals that Okie (presumably at the Behrends' request) did not provide interior designs. This was most likely a cost-saving measure on the part of the owners. Although the correspondence does not reveal Okie's thinking, the building appears to have design features that suggest use as a colonial-era stable or barn.

SMALL BARN AND LARGE BARN

Two existing barns were part of the central core of Glenhill buildings. One located on the circular driveway close to the house was variously referred to in the correspondence as the "small barn," "recreation barn," "bunk house," or "bunk house barn." The alterations included a stone foundation, a large fireplace and chimney, doors, a transom, windows, a staircase, bathrooms, and a sleeping room with "bunks." It provided lodging during the 1930s, when the Behrends entertained large numbers of guests, and it was where Harriet entertained friends. In later years, it also served as a painting studio for Mrs. Behrend.

Garage and farmer's office. Looking southeast from the house, this old photograph shows the five-bay garage with its two apartments for the chauffeurs at the far end. To the right is the farmer's office. (Courtesy Penn State Behrend Archives.)

Garage, north facade. This is the north side of the garage as it appears today. (Photograph by the author.)

The large barn (see page 6), located to the north of the residence, seems not to have been altered with Okie designs, although several drawings in the state archives suggest that alterations were considered, including some that would have added substantial space for living quarters. The large barn housed a number of horses, and a riding ring was built on its east side to serve equestrian activities (Lane 1998, 25).

Small barn before alterations. Viewed from the house, this shows the small barn as it appeared in 1932 prior to being altered. (Courtesy Penn State Behrend Archives.)

Small barn, altered. From a similar vantage point as the previous photograph, this shows the barn with Okie modifications. The barn has a traditional appearance with a stone foundation, a door with antique hardware, windows, transom, and oversized fireplace and chimney—just visible at the upper right (the man and woman are not identified). (Courtesy Penn State Behrend Archives.)

THE CHAPEL IN WINTERGREEN GORGE CEMETERY

Unlike the cluster of residential buildings and outbuildings that were in close proximity, the chapel is located about two-thirds of a mile southwest of the residence in the Wintergreen Gorge Cemetery. The cemetery and the Behrends' property were separated by Four Mile Creek. That area of the creek, with its dramatically steep banks, was known as Wintergreen Gorge or Wintergreen Gulch.

As Okie was designing the chapel in late 1932, the Behrends were making plans for a long-term lease from the cemetery for the land on which the chapel would be built (Behrend Family Collection, folder 1.1.11). The death of their son, Warren, in November 1929 had been devastating to the family, and the chapel was intended to serve as a memorial and burial place for Warren and subsequently for other family members (Lane 1998, 17).

The process of designing and building the chapel was anything but a straightforward affair. Okie had not been the Behrends' first choice as a chapel architect, and some previously existing commitments needed to be clarified and settled before he could get to work on the structure. During October, November, and December 1932, as the original Glenhill residence was being completed, eighteen letters appear in the Okie collection on the subject of Horace Peaslee, the original chapel architect who was based in Washington, DC. Letters were received or sent not only to Mr. Behrend, Okie, and Peaslee but also to Dr. Warren Powers Laird, dean of the School of Architecture at the University of Pennsylvania, and Mr. Behrend's employee Spencer Gordon. These letters comprise the most contentious and emotional topic to be found within the Okie-Behrend file, and although they have no direct bearing on the residential construction, it is clear that this matter was the cause of considerable distress to Mr. and Mrs. Behrend.

Peaslee had been retained by the Behrends to design a chapel well before they engaged Okie. This would have been shortly after Warren's death. The letters reveal that construction on the Peaslee-designed chapel had begun and had then been halted at the Behrends' order. The crux of the problem was that the Behrends had decided that the Peaslee design was not satisfactory, and they wanted to have Okie replace him and create a different design. The sticking point was that the bill Peaslee had submitted had not been fully paid. Spencer Gordon, Mr. Behrend's assistant, had advised the Behrends on the matter—he thought Peaslee's bill was too high. According to the architects' professional code, Okie could not take on the job unless the agreement with the prior architect had been satisfactorily terminated; it had not been, since Peaslee was not willing to waive the unpaid bill, although he offered to lower it.

Okie and Peaslee exchanged letters, with Peaslee explaining his position, making reference to the code of the American Institute of Architects:

> I have made three sets of plans for the Erie chapel over a period of more than two years. The third and last of these plans—working drawings, not preliminary studies—were developed on definite and specific instructions, stage by stage. To date, settlement has not been made for the service rendered, although I have full confidence that Mr. Behrend will in due course make such settlement.
>
> As a member of the Institute, you are of course familiar with the proper procedure in taking over a commission; but I nevertheless appreciate your courtesy in raising the question with me. As soon as "the original relation has been fairly and properly terminated," I will promptly advise you so that you may be free to proceed. I sincerely hope that you will be able to help the Behrends find that for which they are seeking. (Horace Peaslee to Okie, November 9, 1932, Okie Papers)

Spencer Gordon had fired Peaslee on behalf of Mr. Behrend. Gordon requested that Dr. Laird from the University of Pennsylvania arbitrate the dispute. However, Dr. Laird believed that the wisest route was that "negotiations be first made directly between Mr. Behrend and Mr. Peaslee." Dr. Laird continued,

> It would be better if the matter could be settled directly and in the hope that this may be done I defer any proposal of services as an arbitrator. (Laird to Gordon, October 20, 1932, Okie Papers)

It becomes clear that Mr. Behrend was not inclined to take Dr. Laird's advice to deal directly with Peaslee. Rather, he enlisted Okie to try to convince Dr. Laird to "interview Mr. Peaslee and endeavor to make a settlement with him." Ultimately, Peaslee wrote a lengthy, heartfelt letter to Mr. Behrend (it appears that his previous dealings had been with Gordon or Mr. Behrend's secretary). Peaslee gave a detailed review of his bill and the work that he did for it. The total amount he requested was $417; he has been informed that Mr. Behrend had offered to pay Dr. Laird $500 to arbitrate the dispute. Peaslee wrote,

> It doesn't seem worthwhile for either of us to become involved in a possible $500 arbitration fee over an outside difference of about the same amount. You can perhaps afford to do this but in these hard times I cannot. If it were not for these economic conditions, I would be far more concerned about the loss of your confidence which I feel is far more unwarranted. I wish that you had permitted me to step out of the picture when I told you at our last meeting that I had reached that stage. (Peaslee to Mr. Behrend, December 6, 1932, Okie Papers)

This letter from Peaslee clearly struck a nerve and drew an immediate response from Mr. Behrend, who wrote back—in fact, he wrote a letter on each of two consecutive days—addressing Peaslee directly for the first time. One of these letters is noteworthy in that it is by far the longest letter authored by Ernst Behrend in the Okie files. Mr. Behrend was swayed by Peaslee's letter and was willing to pay him. Misunderstanding by Gordon seems to have led to the Behrends' confusion. Mr. Behrend lays some of the blame with Gordon while also taking a swipe at Peaslee with some cryptic comments regarding the poor quality of his work:

> Neither Mrs. Behrend nor I understood that your services rendered in these personal matters had not been paid for and we are naturally anxious to compensate you. Won't you, therefore, send us your bill now covering such service as you have mentioned? . . .
> Neither Mrs. Behrend nor I have been well and I have been under extraordinary and continuous pressure with other matters. I, therefore, have leaned completely on Mr. Gordon. I am not now "passing the buck," but I am simply explaining to you that Mr. Gordon did not understand

your bill and that he considered it excessive, basing his opinion on the accomplishment by you. . . .

When your last drawings came, we were more disappointed than we have been able to tell you. We had expected to be able to proceed but instead had to begin all over again. Did you really think yourself that your last proposition would have produced a satisfactory chapel for the purpose intended? Nobody here thought so. . . .

I am unable to decide matters of this kind, and it has placed a great mental strain upon me. It is for all these reasons that we, in our earnest wish to have justice done, and on Mr. Gordon's suggestion, asked Dr. Laird to tell us what is right. At the time it seemed to us to be the only way to settle the matter. (December 9, 1932, Okie Papers)

With Mr. Behrend's change of heart, the dispute with Horace Peaslee was settled in the architect's favor. Okie took over as the architect for the chapel, and in 1933, progress on it was rapid and to the satisfaction of all concerned. Horace Peaslee continued on with what had been, and what continued to be, a successful career in Washington. His lengthy obituary from May 19, 1959, in the *Washington Post* referred to him as a "nationally known architect whose works included several of the Capital's prominent landmarks." Among his works were the Meridian Hill Park and the Peruvian Embassy in Washington, and landscaping for both the Marine Corps War Memorial in Arlington and President Eisenhower's home in Gettysburg, Pennsylvania. The obituary continues, "Known for his warm personality and gentle wit, Peaslee was a tireless worker in the field of civic and professional activity" (*Washington Post* 1959, B2). His "misunderstanding" with the Behrends appears to have been an exception in an otherwise successful career.

Although the style and design of Horace Peaslee's chapel are unknown, the inspiration for the chapel that Okie built is unmistakable. The chapel in the Wintergreen Gorge Cemetery drew its inspiration from Okie's home church—St. David's Episcopal Church in the Philadelphia suburb of Wayne. The original portion of St. David's was built in 1715 by Welsh colonists and named after the patron saint of Wales (St. David's Episcopal Church, n.d.). Certainly Okie intended the chapel

Chapel, 1934. This photograph shows the newly completed chapel. (Courtesy Pennsylvania State Archives.)

St. David's Episcopal Church, Wayne, Pennsylvania. Okie was an active member of this church, which was built in 1715. Similarities to the Behrend chapel suggest that it served as a source of inspiration in design. (Courtesy St. David's Church.)

to reflect this early colonial architecture, and the two buildings share obvious similarities.

The chapel was put out to bid in the spring of 1933, and construction began that summer. The building was largely completed by fall, although issues regarding interior details and decorations dragged on for many months.

As with other construction at Glenhill, Okie urged the Behrends to make use of contractors and "mechanics" for the chapel whom he recommended. These were men with whom Okie had worked on other projects and had been found to be highly skilled, reliable, and reasonable in cost. They included the mill owner and carpenter Harold Hipple from Harrisburg and the mason DeYenno from Devon. Okie scholar James Garrison describes Okie's close relationship with a small group of contractors: "The contractors and subs understood the project requirements, and over the years, the architect built a strong network with the various trades, ensuring a consistency in the execution of his work" (Garrison 2013, 138). It is clear from his reaction to these suggestions that Mr. Behrend preferred to use local Erie contractors.

Okie's letter from February 6, 1933, in regard to chapel construction—more than any other letter in the correspondence—outlines his desires and rationale in this area. At this point, it had already been made clear that the Behrends were leaning toward a local contractor, while Okie continued to make the case for Hipple to at least do the millwork. From Okie's point of view, Hipple would provide both superior workmanship and superior materials.

> Mr. Hipple . . . has found a very old grist mill in which there are some good oak timbers. In one of the out-buildings there is some additional lumber that has been cut and stored for quite a number of years.
>
> I have been anxious to get Mr. Hipple to furnish the window and door frames and the interior woodwork for the Chapel, having the same made in his shop where a great deal of the work is done by hand. Will you let me order the Chapel frames, pews, pulpits, etc., from Mr. Hipple, letting his men prepare the material during the next few weeks when it will be

possible to have them do the work at a price that is quite a little less per hour than has been customary. . . .

There would be a decided advantage in having the thoroughly seasoned material used and in having the work done by Mr. Hipple's mechanics, who are thoroughly familiar with our drawings and the effect we are trying to get. From past experiences I have found Mr. Hipple and his organization to be most conscientious in putting millwork together, making all mortise and tenons fits, etc. accurately and using plenty of white lead in the joints. In addition to this, they understand how the material is to be planed by hand rather than any machine work which adds very much to the effect of the finished product without unreasonable additional expense.

Interestingly, in the final paragraph of this letter, Okie referred to problems that had surfaced in the Behrends' new house as the result of a less demanding approach to materials and labor; this was a reference to either leaks that had developed or problems with some floor boards, both of which are mentioned elsewhere in the correspondence:

In fact, there may be a little saving in connection with the millwork and there will not be the trouble with shrinkage, etc. that we are now experiencing in your house at the farm. (Okie to Mr. Behrend, Okie Papers)

The general contract for the chapel went to the Henry Shenk Company of Erie (whereas the work on the house and other buildings was done by Sessinghaus and Ostergaard, also of Erie). However, as Okie recommended, the chapel millwork was done by Harold Hipple of Harrisburg and the masonry was the responsibility, all or in part, of DeYenno and a small crew of men who traveled with him from Devon.

In late 1933, as chapel construction was well under way, William Okie wrote to the Henry Shenk Company. His letter provides further evidence of the attention to detail that he and his brother gave to their projects and is not atypical of other letters wherein they call on the contractors to meet their requirements:

We wish you to proceed with the cellar door and . . . are enclosing a sketch covering the same. You will notice the boards are tongued, grooved and beaded, and that the doors are rabbeted as suggested when I was in Erie. Will you please see that these doors are made of genuine Michigan White Pine and that they are thoroughly leaded between all joints. . . .

When in Erie, I intended to speak to you about the chancel sub-floor. This is specified Long Leaf Georgia Yellow Pine and, if I am not mistaken, you have used something that is no better than North Carolina. If this is so, will you please put down the good sub-floor before the finished floor is laid. (William Okie to Henry Shenk, December 29, 1933, Okie Papers)

The chapel is unique among Okie's Glenhill buildings in that it was built on land that the Behrends did not own. Rather, they leased the property from the cemetery. In the late 1930s and 1940s, Mrs. Behrend corresponded with Okie in regard to several chapel topics including dampness in the building, the need for a stone wall around the property, and the issue of the local boys breaking the windows. In the early 1950s, when the lease

Chapel in winter. The monument on the right is the memorial to the Behrend's son, Warren, who died in an automobile accident in 1929. (Courtesy Penn State Behrend Archives.)

Chapel in summer. This photograph presents a view from the southwest. (Photograph by the author.)

of the land was due to expire, Mrs. Behrend negotiated not to renew it but to have the Wintergreen Gorge Cemetery take over the maintenance (Erie Cemetery 1953). Over the subsequent decades, other members of the Behrend family have been interred in the chapel, and members of their extended family and close friends were buried nearby. Meanwhile, the Penn State community created and maintained a strong connection with the chapel through the college's Hanging of the Greens ceremony, which is held there each December.

CHAPTER FIVE

The Economics of Glenhill Farm

The building of the Glenhill estate was an expensive undertaking that touched many people, including the clients, the architect and his staff, contractors, laborers, and numerous vendors. Economic and financial issues are naturally a part of any large construction effort, but because this project began as the country headed into the worst years of the Great Depression, some of the economic issues were particularly salient. One example of this touched on previously was Horace Peaslee's reference to "these hard times." Other letters throughout the correspondence contain references to financial issues, which typically involve several themes. These include many routine business matters such as bids, cost estimates, and bills; suggestions on ways to economize on the construction through changes in design or the use of alternative materials; and allusions to the difficult economic times affecting the nation.

The cost associated with the construction of Glenhill Farm is a thread that runs throughout the correspondence. The first and last letters in the voluminous files are somewhat typical. In the very first letter in 1931, Spencer Gordon worried that he was asking Brognard Okie to provide labor and sketches beyond what Mr. Behrend had agreed to pay for. In the last two letters, thirteen years later, Mrs. Behrend and Okie had difficulty resolving a final bill. Throughout the correspondence, there are frequent examples of what might be described as a mild tug of war between clients and architect—the former wanting to be economical and the latter wanting to maintain quality. Okie certainly had standards that he strove to uphold in regard to his designs, the caliber of materials, and the excellent construction of the Glenhill buildings. While he wanted to be economical with the Behrends' money and many times acceded to their suggestions for economizing, there were instances when he would insist on doing it his way. An example of this type of interaction is illustrated here as Mrs. Behrend wrote to Okie about a new version of a house plan:

> We believe we could use stock door frames particularly in the servants' rooms, and in fact, all through the house, if possible. We want to cut down the cost in every way and still have the house as attractive and as simple as possible. (April 10, 1933, Okie Papers)

As one might suspect, the proposal of "stock door frames" did not meet Okie's standards, yet typical of him, he responded in a diplomatic fashion:

> I will get an estimate on the interior and exterior millwork . . . from one or two millmen here to compare with the figures that your contractor gives you in Erie as I am most anxious not to use the stock material that you speak of. By getting one of the mills that do a good deal of work for us and who have cutters for their machines to fit the different moulds that we design, there will be very little difference in cost between the stock material and material following our drawings. (April 13, 1933, Okie Papers)

Although Okie incorporated a number of Mrs. Behrend's recommendations regarding the interior layout of the house, he held the line on several of her suggestions regarding the exterior. To her proposal that a chimney be placed on the outside wall of the house as a way to save money, Okie replied,

> Livingroom chimney projecting beyond wall spoils elevation suggest widening living room eighteen inches making main portion house longer this no more expensive than projecting chimney please advise. (Telegram, May 9, 1932, as quoted in Mr. Behrend's letter of May 10, Okie Papers)

The final results often reflected a compromise. In the case of the chimneys, they remained on the interior of the house. The millwork and masonry reflect a mix: some buildings reflect custom work by Hipple and DeYenno, while others were the work of local laborers.

It is estimated that the total cost for property and building came to about $300,000 (M. Behrend 1943). The correspondence indicates that the cost of the construction exceeded $150,000, which can be accounted for approximately as follows: modifications to the Schley house and garage, $6,000; main house and shelter shed, $108,000; garage, $15,000; chapel, $19,000; bathhouse, unknown. Additional cost was no doubt incurred for buildings and other construction, such as the swimming pool, tennis court, bridle paths, and landscaping. These were not worked on by Okie and therefore not reflected in the correspondence. In today's dollars, the cost of the buildings and property would be the equivalent of more than $5 million (United States Department of Labor, n.d.).

The Behrends' ability to pay for their new estate at a time when the nation was heading into troubled economic times is a theme that is touched on in the correspondence. Between 1916 and 1932, the Hammermill Paper Company realized considerable success. In spite of the stock market crash of 1929, the company enjoyed record profits that year (McQuillen and Garvey 1985, 78). The Behrends owned the vast majority of Hammermill stock, and to say that they were wealthy may be an understatement. In addition to the value of their stockholdings, Mr. Behrend earned a salary in excess of $250,000 per year, or about $4.3 million in today's dollars. In contrast, one of Harold Hipple's "better" carpenters who traveled from Harrisburg to work on Glenhill was paid $1 an hour—or about $2,000 per year—which was the generally accepted minimum budget for a family of four at that time (Goldberg 2003, 128). To put it another way, Mr. Behrend's annual salary was 125 times greater than one of Glenhill's skilled laborers.

Two of the Behrends' purchases in 1928 and 1929 serve to illustrate the nature of their wealth. In 1929, Mr. Behrend made final payment on a new yacht that was built for him in 1928. It was 195 feet long and was constructed by the Krupp Corporation in Germany (M. Behrend 1943). In today's dollars, the yacht cost well over $5 million to build and, requiring a crew of thirty-two, more than $500,000 a year to maintain (Lindsay

1943). Their purchase of a 1929 Duesenberg, the most expensive car on the American market at that time, would have cost somewhere between $190,000 and $260,000 in today's dollars (Wikipedia 2018).

By 1932, as the Depression deepened, Hammermill's business dropped dramatically. Paper prices were way down, demand was slow, and production was drastically reduced (McQuillen and Garvey 1985, 85). In deciding against building the house on the hill in February 1933, Mr. Behrend was not exaggerating when he wrote that "business is in such a condition, we had to lay off so many people . . . while my income decreases" (Mr. Behrend to Okie, February 3, 1933, Okie Papers).

Another indication of the difficult economic times is reflected in the letters between Okie and various contractors and vendors. For example, a large number of unsolicited letters and brochures were sent directly to Okie from suppliers and contractors looking for work and sales. These businessmen had gotten word of the work at Glenhill and were hoping to get some of the action. For the house, these included vendors of kitchen equipment, interior decorators, plasterers, fireplace equipment suppliers, and custom woodworkers. For the chapel, these included makers of religious furnishings, altar cloths, candelabras, and stained-glass windows, to name a few. Further evidence of the hard times is found in a letter from Harold Hipple, the contractor and lumber specialist whom Okie relied on for securing and milling antique lumber. In the spring of 1933, Hipple expressed to Okie his hope that the Behrends would have more work for him. He conveyed a sense of desperation as he wrote that he was "trying to keep my little mill together."

In early 1933, in a letter to Mr. Behrend, Okie urges him to put the chapel out to bid. Nationwide unemployment for the Depression years peaked in 1933 at 25 percent, and the nation's income had dropped by half of what it had been only a few years earlier (Carson and Bonk 1999, 394). Okie was clearly sympathetic to the plight of the workers. He was also aware that it presented an excellent opportunity to get a low bid due to the desperate times. He reminded Mr. Behrend of both of these Depression-era realities:

> I feel it is a great pity to postpone the taking of estimates at this time when the mere fact of letting the local contractors, whom you want to figure on the building, know that there is some work in prospect will be an

encouragement to them; besides which I am sure that you would get very advantageous estimates on the building if we could send the drawings out now. (January 28, 1933, Okie Papers)

Mr. Behrend ultimately agreed with Okie, and the chapel construction went out to bid a short time later. Reflecting the difficult times, nine contractors submitted a bid, and in a letter to Mrs. Behrend, Okie remarked that it was an unexpectedly high number:

We had such an unusual number of contractors to whom plans and specifications had to be sent that I am unable to send Mr. Behrend and you a set of the completed drawings at this time, but I will do so as soon as possible. (March 10, 1933, Okie Papers)

At the same time that the Behrends were reviewing near-final plans for the two large additions to the house, Mr. Behrend shared his concern about the national economy in an essay in the company newsletter. The *Hammermill Bond*, the publication that had been suspended in 1930 for financial reasons, was back in print as of December 22, 1933. He wrote,

The Hammermill Bond suspended for reasons of economy, reappears at a time when President Roosevelt is making the greatest possible effort to end an economic depression such as this country has never before known. . . . The reissue of The Hammermill Bond does not mean that prosperity has returned to us; it does mean that we wish to reestablish the means of communication and the exchange of ideas which The Bond always has so well provided in the past. It seems fitting that the first number should come out at Christmas time, a season when our faith in mankind and our hope for the future should be at high tide. Great problems and difficulties still lie before us. I have no doubt that united, with honest individual effort, and with fairness and justice to each other, we shall successfully solve them. (E. Behrend 1933)

CHAPTER SIX

Life at Glenhill in the 1930s

As Mr. Behrend indicated in a letter to Brognard Okie, the first time that the family slept in the Glenhill Farmhouse (the original "cottage" version) was during Thanksgiving week of 1932 with Harriet home from college—and they were delighted with the house. During the next eight years, the family would spend much of their time at the new estate. However, their interests and activities were such that during most years, they spent considerable time away from Glenhill.

In both 1933 and 1934, long vacations to California and Arizona took them away for the coldest months of the year. Furthermore, the construction of the two additions precluded their full-time occupancy until late 1934. In 1935, six weeks in February and March were spent in Central and South America touring and meeting with Hammermill agents in various countries, including Cuba, Peru, Argentina, Brazil, and Chile. During the first four months of 1937, a world cruise took them to the far reaches of the globe, including Africa and Asia. A new home in Sea Island, Georgia, was a regular destination for escaping the Erie winters.

In spite of their absence during the cold-weather months, Glenhill was their home, and while the letters between the Behrends and Okie do not provide much description of life at Glenhill, archival materials in the Behrend Family Collection give some indication of how they spent their time. Personal letters, scrapbooks and photographs, a family guest book, and information from the *Hammermill Bond* help provide a glimpse into life at Glenhill in the 1930s.

Although semiretired, Mr. Behrend remained active in the company. As Mrs. Behrend noted, when he returned home from his morning trip to the plant, he often brought one or two guests to join them for lunch. Ernst continued his interest and leadership in community affairs, serving on the boards of a local hospital, the Community Chest, and the Deerfield Academy (in Massachusetts), where his son, Warren, had been a student. An avid chess player, Mr. Behrend was heavily involved with the Erie Chess Club. In the mid-1930s, he was honored with an honorary doctorate from Thiel College in Greenville, Pennsylvania, and was appointed a trustee of the Institute of Paper Chemistry in Appleton, Wisconsin.

Mrs. Behrend participated in charitable works and spent time gardening, oil painting, and raising prize-winning dogs. The Behrends' daughter, Harriet, shared her parents' interest in canines, entering her dogs in shows where she won awards. She also achieved acclaim as an equestrian and made active use of a large riding ring that was built on the east side of the large barn. Another talent at which she excelled was skeet shooting, for which she won national awards in the early 1940s. In all, Glenhill Farm in

Mr. Behrend and friends. In 1933, on the east side of the house, Mr. Behrend holds the attention of one German shepherd, three poodles, and a Doberman pinscher. (Courtesy Penn State Behrend Archives.)

the mid- and late 1930s was a hub of entertainment and dining with guests from around the globe. Activities included horseback riding; dog raising; maintaining horses, sheep, and goats; gardening; painting; tennis; swimming; and playing chess. The estate served as a point of departure for the family's long cruises around the world and for winter travel to Arizona, California, and Georgia.

In the architectural drawing for the 1934 additions to Glenhill, a room on the first floor of the service wing is labeled "Boy's Bedroom." The quarters include a fireplace, private bath, and door to a small porch. The "boy" referred to one of Mr. Behrend's personal secretaries, Frank Knauer, who authored several letters found in Okie's files. Frank was twenty-three years old in 1934 and had been on Mr. Behrend's personal payroll and had lived with the family since 1931. Years later, Knauer reminisced about various aspects of life at Glenhill during the 1930s. For instance, he recalled how the Behrends hosted annual Christmas parties for all the children in the neighborhood. Held in the small barn, the parties drew a large crowd of children and their parents and included a program

Mrs. Behrend, spring 1933. Near the large barn and the new corral, Mrs. Behrend poses with a young goat. (Courtesy Penn State Behrend Archives.)

Mrs. Behrend the artist. One of Mrs. Behrend's hobbies was painting. This guestbook entry by noted Erie artist Joseph Plavcan shows her at work, most likely in the small barn that she is known to have used as a studio. This painting is dated 1945, and the inscription at the bottom left, above Plavcan's signature, reads, "Glenhill Art Center. Summer school 1945. We tried desperately to center." Plavcan served as Mrs. Behrend's painting tutor. (Courtesy Penn State Behrend Archives.)

Guests at the pool, September 1934. The Behrends hosted a large party shortly after moving into Glenhill as fulltime occupants. Some of the guests are seen in this photo. Entertainment included a troop of gymnasts from the local YMCA. (Photograph by Henry E. Obermanns, courtesy Penn State Behrend Archives.)

and a treasure hunt (Knauer, n.d.). Knauer was "treated almost as one of the family," taking many of his meals with the Behrends, including summer lunches at the pool-side picnic table under the slowly turning fan and often attending Harriet's parties held for her friends in the small barn.

One of Frank's special remembrances was the two-month trip that he took with the Behrends in the winter of 1934 to Arizona and California, traveling by train and enjoying a luxurious lifestyle. While at the Arrowhead Springs Hotel, he enjoyed the warm weather, went horseback riding, lunched with the Behrends and famous guests at the pool, and "enjoyed black tie dinners each night" (Stachelek 2004, 10). The Behrends were very fond of Frank, and he speculated that the loss of their son, Warren, in late 1929 may have led Mr. and Mrs. Behrend to view him as something of a surrogate son.

The Behrend family photo albums from the 1930s strongly reflect the important role that animals played in the lives of the family members.

Frank Knauer's diving skills. Mr. Behrend's protégé and Glenhill resident Frank Knauer displays his skills at the September 1934 event. (Photograph by Henry E. Obermanns, courtesy Penn State Behrend Archives.)

Family photographs show Harriet and Ernst on horseback, Mary with a young goat, and both Ernst and Harriet with their favorite canine companions. Looking back on the 1930s at Glenhill, Mrs. Behrend reflected,

> We spent many wonderful years here. There were long walks in the woods and always the dogs were with us. We had many dogs. At one time a sign on the East Drive read "Please drive slowly—16 dogs." Of course, this was counting the puppies! (M. Behrend 1958)

Harriet at Glenhill Farm, 1932. (Courtesy Penn State Behrend Archives.)

Mr. Behrend and Harriet on horseback. Skilled equestrians, father and daughter pose near the large barn in spring 1932. (Courtesy Penn State Behrend Archives.)

Mrs. Behrend's description of life at Glenhill continued with some of their social activities:

> We had picnics and barbecues and once a year a big Hammermill carnival with games and speeches. Almost every day Mr. Behrend would bring an extra man or two out for lunch at the long table by the pool. Business men appeared from many places. All over the world it seemed as Hammermill paper was used in Barbados, China, Cuba and many other places. We also entertained old people from the different charitable homes in Erie. I remember we gave each one flowers to take home. Often thirty or more bouquets were sent in town for the District Nurses to distribute. (M. Behrend 1958)

The Behrends maintained a unique guestbook—oversized and bound in brown leather with gilt lettering on the front that reads "Glenhill 1932." This guestbook contains at least a partial record of the friends and other visitors whom they entertained. Judging from the nature of the numerous entries, the guests must have been encouraged to display their creativity in the form of a poem or rhyme and a drawing if they were up to it. Colored pencils and crayons must have been kept nearby, as these thank-yous make a vibrant and attractive form of remembrance. Naturally, the entries represent three seasons of the year—fall, spring, and summer—since the Behrends were absent during the winter months. The first entry in the guestbook was penned during the inaugural week of Glenhill, 1932, when one of their dinner guests wrote,

> I came to the Farm for Thanksgiving Dinner,
> And when I leave, although much less thinner,
> I've a blackened eye and a broken nose
> And a great desire for complete repose.
>   (Behrend Family Guestbook 1932)

Other entries in the guestbook reflect a sense of the Behrends' interests. As might be expected, Mrs. Behrend's devotion to gardening is evident, with several garden clubs being entertained for lunch, including twenty members of the Junior League Garden Club in the summer of 1933. And for several consecutive years, as many as sixteen guests stayed overnight in August for the Erie Horse Show, an event with which the family was closely involved.

One of the historically unique marketing features of the Hammermill Paper Company was its use of exclusive franchised jobbers (McQuillen and Garvey 1985, 52). For decades, these agents had been invited each summer to attend the Hammermill Conference in Erie, and of the 130 or so who attended, a select group—the "advisory committee"—of approximately 20 guests was invited to stay with the Behrends at the farm in the 1930s. Their signatures in the guestbook at this late-August event reflect their geographic diversity from around the country and around the globe.

A Glenhill visitor who in later years would achieve international acclaim was Raoul Wallenberg. At the time of his first visit with the Behrends in July 1933, Wallenberg was just about to turn twenty-one years old. He had met the Behrends at the Chicago World's Fair earlier in the year. Born into Sweden's leading family of financiers, Wallenberg had come to the United States to study architecture at the University of Michigan. Later, in 1944, he would achieve international fame as a hero of World War II with his efforts to save the lives of many Hungarian Jews from Nazi extermination (Jangfeldt 2012, 1). Letters that he wrote to his family reveal that he visited the Behrends at least twice. Furthermore, it appears that the Behrends asked him to review some of Okie's drawings for the residence in late 1933, a time period that would have corresponded with the nearly final drawings for the additions to the house. In a letter to his grandfather back in Sweden, Raoul Wallenberg wrote, "The Behrends in Erie are building a large house and they . . . had me look through the building plans to see if they might be improved upon" (Wallenberg 1995, 9).

Another interesting entry in the Glenhill guestbook was penned by Elizabeth Pattee and Constance Peters. These two women maintained an architectural and landscape design firm in Boston, and Elizabeth Pattee had done landscape architectural work for another of the Behrends' homes in Newport, Rhode Island, some years before (Allaback 2008, 167). Although Arthur Cowell of State College had been retained as the original landscape architect for Glenhill, it is unclear how extensive his involvement

Guestbook entry of Raoul Wallenberg. From July 1933, this black crayon drawing by Wallenberg seems to show him (RW) looking toward an urban skyline. This may be a reference to Raoul's avocation of hitch-hiking throughout the United States. Underneath in bold letters, the words "Magnificent Herring Salad" is likely a tribute to the Behrends' excellent cuisine and perhaps a favorite dish of his. Wallenberg's signature is at the bottom right. (Courtesy Penn State Behrend Archives.)

was. It is clear, however, from letters and blueprints in the Okie file that in 1933, Pattee and Peters had been retained by the Behrends to oversee the landscaping of the new estate, including the walkways near the house, Mrs. Behrend's garden, and the orchard of fruit trees. The guestbook entry reveals that they stayed at Glenhill for ten days in August 1933 while conducting some of their work. Like so many of the Behrends' guests, they provided an interesting documentation of their stay, with images of a walkway and them at work with some of the tools of their trade—a tape measure, rule, stake, and mallet.

A topic of conversation around the Behrend dinner table in the 1930s must have been the adventures of Paul A. Siple. Once known as the "world's most famous Boy Scout," Siple was an Erie resident and Eagle Scout who at age nineteen was selected from among six hundred thousand scouts by Admiral Richard Byrd to accompany his expeditions to the South Pole beginning in 1928 and continuing over the next decades (*New*

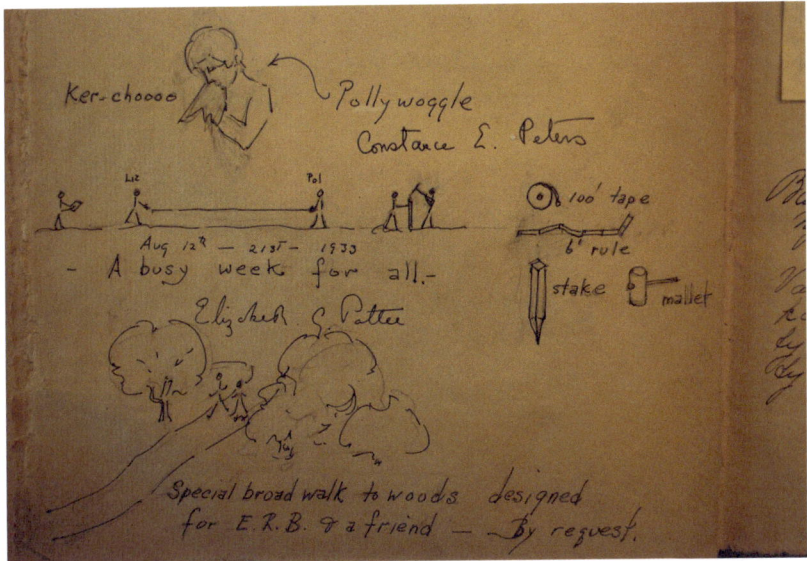

Visit from the landscape architects. This August 1933 entry in the Glenhill guestbook confirms a visit by Constance Peters and Elizabeth Pattee, partners in an architectural firm in Boston. Clearly they had been hard at work during their stay with the Behrends. Perhaps Constance suffered from a cold or hay fever? (Courtesy Penn State Behrend Archives.)

York Times 1968, 7). He may well have been a dinner guest at Glenhill. Clearly the Behrends were acquainted with Siple, as the *Hammermill Bond* reported that he borrowed Mr. Behrend's sextant for several of these polar expeditions (*Hammermill Bond* 1939, 5). Presumably this was a sextant that Mr. Behrend used aboard his yacht, the *Amida*. Siple became a leading expert on Antarctica, and as a distinguished scientist, he is credited with coining the term *wind-chill factor* in his 1939 geography dissertation, a concept that he codeveloped with Charles Passel (*USA Today* 2001).

Undoubtedly one of the most noteworthy events ever held at Glenhill occurred in the summer of 1938. That year, the *Hammermill Bond* published a fifteen-page special issue reporting on a daylong celebration of the company's fortieth anniversary held on the Glenhill estate: "Promptly at 8:30 o'clock that morning of June twenty-fifth the caravan of over six hundred automobiles moved out of Hammermill road and paraded with banners and sound trucks to the site of the celebration in a grove on Glenhill farm. The out-door auditorium with its benches for all made an impressive

Harriet with a police escort. On the day of the fortieth anniversary of the Hammermill Paper Company, Harriet Behrend speaks with police as they prepare to escort a caravan of six hundred cars from the plant to Glenhill Farm for the celebration. (Photograph by Henry E. Obermanns, courtesy Penn State Behrend Archives.)

Gathered for the fortieth anniversary. Hammermill employees are gathered for a program of speeches on the hillside not far from the Glenhill residence. (Photograph by Henry E. Obermanns, courtesy Penn State Behrend Archives.)

Mr. Behrend, 1930s. In this undated photograph, likely from the mid-1930s, Mr. Behrend is seen taking some refreshment. Although the location is probably at the Hammermill plant, a similar photograph might easily have been taken at Glenhill during one of the several large employee celebrations that were held there in the summers throughout the decade. (Courtesy Penn State Behrend Archives.)

setting for the formal program which began shortly after ten and lasted until noon" (*Hammermill Bond* 1938, 3). Seating for the fifteen hundred employees in attendance was provided on the gently sloping hillside to the west of the residence, not far from the area that is now known as the college picnic grove. The report continues, "Mr. Ernst R. Behrend, president of Hammermill and co-founder with his brother, Dr. Otto F. Behrend, of the nation's best-known fine writing paper mill, was principal speaker at the fortieth anniversary commemoration and service program" (3). Otto and Mary Behrend also spoke to the crowd, after which a picnic ensued, with food and games with prizes taking up the rest of the memorable day. During several other years in the 1930s, the company newsletter reported on picnic celebrations hosted by the Behrends at Glenhill to honor about three hundred employees each year; those were large celebrations indeed, but the grand and historic fortieth anniversary celebration was a "topic of conversation for many a day to come" (3).

CHAPTER SEVEN

The Late Correspondence

By late 1935, correspondence between the Behrends and Brognard Okie had become less frequent. The buildings were completed, and the Behrends were enjoying their home and grounds. In late 1935 and into early 1936, Mrs. Behrend and Okie corresponded several times on the topic of the placement of her desk and the possibility of making an alteration to accommodate it. She wrote,

> My desk is in my bedroom which makes a continued clutter and a restlessness anyhow. I don't like to take the "office" down stairs as Mr. Behrend really uses it a great deal. Can you squeeze me in a room of any sort—anywhere? I do like the east side best and would like a place for my desk—good light, broad window seat for plants, books, etc., just a small place for work.
>
> I thought possibly you and your brother might be coming this way to see the house, garage, etc. finished. It is all beginning to look very nice and would be glad to have you come and stay overnight—Why not bring your family—We have plenty of beds for all—5 or 6. We have 16 here over the horse show. (September 17, 1935, Okie Papers)

Okie replied to these topics and also made reference to a suggestion that Mrs. Behrend had made regarding the construction of an outdoor sheltered area:

In reply to your recent note, I am working on a suggestion for a change in your house that will provide a desk room and will have a drawing ready to send you within a few days. . . .

Regarding the shelter over the entrance gate—I am disappointed to hear the suggestion . . . as it seems to me any glass enclosure of the arbor would be thoroughly out of keeping with the house and most unfortunate. . . .

My brother and I have been hoping that we could go to Erie to see Mr. Behrend and you and look at the completed house and other buildings but it has been impossible for us to do so, first one reason and then another. . . .

It is very kind of you to think of asking us to take our families with us when we go to Erie and I am sure both my brother's wife and mine would enjoy the trip immensely. (September 25, 1935, Okie Papers)

In 1939, Okie worked to address the Behrends' concern about dampness in the chapel, and he exchanged letters with them and with contractors in an attempt to resolve the problem. Also in 1939, Mrs. Behrend requested his advice on the possibility of installing an elevator or an "inclinator" in the house to make it easier to get from one floor to the other. Mr. Behrend had suffered a heart attack, and she wanted to make an alteration that would make things easier for him.

In early 1940, Mrs. Behrend and Okie exchanged several letters. The Behrends were staying at their winter home at Cottage 92, Sea Island, Georgia. Mrs. Behrend had admired a paint color that had been used at Pennsbury Manor, and she had asked Okie to help her obtain the same for use at the cottage. In a detailed letter, he provided a description of the history of the paint color and also described his involvement in this large project that he had overseen a couple of years earlier for the Commonwealth of Pennsylvania:

This was the restoration of William Penn's home on the Delaware, which we recently completed for the Pennsylvania Historical Commission and the General State Authority. I think with one of my previous letters, we sent you a photograph of the sketch of these Pennsbury buildings. . . . This work at Pennsbury comprised not only the Manor House, but the restoration of the Bake and Brew House, Horse Stable . . . a smoke house and ice house. (April 29, 1940, Okie Papers)

Mrs. Behrend replied as follows:

Many thanks for your interesting letter of the 29th of April. I hope we can stop on the way up and see these buildings at Pennsbury. I shall keep your letter to refer to when we are there. . . .

Mr. Behrend is better and looks and seems more like his old self. He has to be a little careful not to overdo. But he says there are many compensations about not rushing about so quickly, trying to do everything at one time. We are all together more, he can read and enjoy the garden—also he finds much of his business can be transacted in a rather comfortable, calm way. He keeps cheerful and occupied. Chess problems take up quite a bit of his time. He sends his kindest regards to you and your brother.

With best wishes to all the Okies from us all (May 1, 1940, Okie Papers)

On May 11, Okie replied, giving Mrs. Behrend detailed driving instructions on getting to Pennsbury, which she had requested, and he concluded,

My brother and I would appreciate it very much if we could meet you in Philadelphia and go to Pennsbury with you. The above directions may be a little confusing for your chauffeur, so we could lead the way. . . . It is fine to hear that Mr. Behrend has improved and I trust he will soon be entirely recovered. (Okie Papers)

The Behrends were not able to take advantage of Okie's offer of a guided tour of Pennsbury Manor. On the stationery of the Barclay Hotel in New York, Mrs. Behrend explained,

Harriet and I motored directly up here and had no time to see Pennsbury. I am keeping your letter with directions how to get there and hope later on I can do this. As I may go on a little antiquing trip thru Penna. and possibly we can visit this interesting place. . . . Mr. Behrend is better and feels encouraged after being able to attend several large meetings here in New York. Thank you for suggesting you would escort us out. (May 23, 1940, Okie Papers)

Based on the evidence of the correspondence, it appears that the Behrends never paid a visit to Pennsbury. Ernst Behrend died a few months later in September 1940 at the age of seventy-one.

The American flag at the Hammermill plant flew at half-mast as the death of Mr. Behrend delivered a blow to family, friends, community members, and the Hammermill employees and retirees. The *Hammermill Bond* devoted the October issue to Ernst's life and accomplishments, a copy of which Mrs. Behrend sent to Brognard and William Okie. The publication noted that many hundreds of people attended the funeral at the Luther Memorial Church in Erie. The *Hammermill Bond* noted that "Perhaps the best testimonial to the life of Mr. Behrend was the complete respect his employees had for him while he lived. . . . One of the Utility Crew boys put it this way: 'Mr. Behrend he was a mighty fine man and my friend. I feel bad—just as bad as I do the day my own father is dead'" (*Hammermill Bond* 1940). His obituary in the *New York Times* highlighted his accomplishments as a business leader and a pioneer in the paper-making industry: "His founding of the first all-sulphite process paper mill in this country marked the start of a new trend in the nation's manufacture of business papers. He was the inventor of high-speed watermarking, one of the paper industry's most important contributions." And he "was one of the nation's pioneers in establishing friendly employee relations between employer and employee" (*New York Times* 1940). Ernst was interred in the chapel built seven years earlier to honor his son, Warren.

Mr. Behrend's death led directly to a couple of issues that would involve Okie. One of these was the possible construction of a wall around the grounds of the chapel. The construction of a wall or fence around the chapel was a topic that went back to the time of its original construction. The Behrends thought that a wall would clearly delineate the Behrend chapel property. However, action had been put off. But now with Mr. Behrend's death and interment in the chapel, it became a concern again. After reviewing plans for a proposed wall that Okie sent in February 1943, Mrs. Behrend replied,

> Your plans for the wall, with the main entrance protected with the roof and seats, are a little more elaborate than I thought of. I would like a low stone wall with a stone coping. I want more than anything to enclose the property so there will be no question about it at any future time. (March 1, 1943, Okie Papers)

Okie had included the contractor, Sessinghaus and Ostergaard, in the conversation about the chapel wall. Ostergaard wrote back to Okie and, in effect, put the brakes on the possibility of the construction of wall, at least for the foreseeable future. He reflected on the practical issues that World War II had on such a project and wrote that Sessinghaus

> has talked to Mrs. Behrend regarding this matter and she seemed to be inclined to defer this work under the present conditions. We, ourselves, doubt very much that permission could be obtained from the War Production Board to go ahead with a project of this nature. . . . Even though practically all the material here involved could be had without a great deal of priority help, the difficulty seems to be getting permission to use man power on non-defense work. (March 8, 1943, Okie Papers)

Ultimately, Mrs. Behrend got her wish. An undated photograph of the chapel in winter shows the "low stone wall with a stone coping" that she desired, although at some point the wall was removed.

In 1943 and 1944, Mrs. Behrend's letterhead read, "Mrs. Mary B. Behrend, 114 West Seventh Street, Erie, Pa." Apparently she had relocated to quarters in the city of Erie. It is known that after Mr. Behrend's death in 1940, Mrs. Behrend started to spend more time at her home in Greenwich, Connecticut (Knauer, n.d.). One of her most interesting letters to Okie was that of January 29, 1944, as she contemplated the difficulties in the world as World War II continued, her own more solitary existence, and a different use for the Glenhill residence. It reads as follows:

Dear Mr. Okie:

This winter I thought I might be in Philadelphia and surely intended to call on you and your brother. I trust you and your family are quite well.

These are strenuous times in the world. We all hope for an early ending of the war. My contribution to the war effort is endeavoring to produce as much as possible in the way of food for the local markets—steers, lambs, chickens, pigs, vegetables, etc. However, should the war cease, I would very quickly reduce all this and I might possibly even travel or be with my sister. I am not sure what plans I would have but at any rate, I would like to have your opinion about the practicability of dividing this house into two dwellings for rental. At the moment there is a scarcity of housing in Erie. This, of course, may not continue, I am not even sure I would want to do this, but I would appreciate it if you could look over the plans and let me know what you think about it.

I felt the back of the house—the ground floor bedroom off the kitchen could be a little living room, and the kitchen could be divided with a kind of dining alcove at the end, and the back upstairs bedrooms—would make one part of the house. This would necessitate another kitchen being put on the first floor in another part of the house. I had even thought of closing off the large living room. I suppose there are various ways this could be arranged and, naturally, I would not want to go into any great expense to do it as it might be well to have it so it could easily— double padded or sound proof doors to be removed—be put back to the original arrangement again.

You see I am quite alone here and it is a large place to keep up. Because of the fact that it is on the east side of the town, it might be difficult to dispose of it but I might be able to rent it if it could be divided up. I would appreciate it very much if I could have your opinion. (Okie Papers)

Later that year, Mrs. Behrend again found a reason to consult the architect—1944 was the three-hundredth anniversary of William Penn's birth, and it was being widely celebrated. The subject of Pennsbury Manor arose again as she wrote,

At a garden club meeting yesterday, the ladies were talking about the William Penn Celebration that all the clubs were to have in October. As I
understand it, it is about the William Penn town that you built up. I told the
president of the garden club that I would write to you and ask if any historical paper had been prepared to be used in connection with this event this
fall. Also, would there be any photographs or pictures of the settlement?
Possibly there is a committee that is arranging all these things. We would
appreciate any suggestions or assistance. (August 10, 1944, Okie Papers)

Throughout twelve years of correspondence between Okie and
Mr. and Mrs. Behrend, the tenor of the letters had always remained cordial and pleasant, and a fondness seems to have developed. The Behrends
had sent gifts to Mrs. Okie, a wedding gift to the Okies' daughter, and
Christmas cards were exchanged. Mrs. Behrend had invited the wives
of both Brognard Okie and William Okie to visit Glenhill with their
husbands and stay for a few days. With this congenial history, the tone
of the final two letters comes as a surprise—the first from Mrs. Behrend.
She has received a bill for Okie's work on the plans for dividing the house
into apartments:

Your letter of September 15, enclosing a bill, has been received. There
surely is some mistake in the bill, which I am returning together with the
blue prints, as these are merely blue prints exactly like I have only with lines
drawn across them, which could not have taken very much time. This is
about the same conclusion I worked out on my own blue prints.

When I wrote to you on January 29, 1944, explaining what I had in
mind, I really only wanted an opinion from you if it would be anything to
consider and I certainly did not intend to give the impression that I wanted
to go ahead with any work or incur *any expense* whatever at that time.

You see, Mr. Okie, it is only an extremely remote possibility that I might
ever want to make such a change and I only felt as you had been associated with us so long that I could always ask your opinion. In the remote
case that I should ever consider doing this, then I would, of course, take
the matter up with you and I would expect at that time that there would

be some expense connected with it. I would never want to spoil anything you had designed by having anyone else come in on it.

> With kind regards to your family (September 21, 1944, Okie Papers)

Normally very prompt in his responses to Mrs. Behrend, in this instance Okie replied nearly a month later. To those who have read his letters to the Behrends, the abbreviated closing "Very sincerely yours," stands in contrast to his customary use of the more elaborate "With kindest regards, I am, very sincerely yours" or previously "With kindest regards to you and Mr. Behrend, I am, very truly yours":

> Your letter of September 21st with which you returned the bill I submitted for services in connection with the suggested changes at your farm was a disappointment to me.
>
> The working out of the plans I sent you and the drafting required several days study and work, and in addition there was a small item of blue printing.
>
> As you can readily appreciate due to war time restrictions, etc. architectural work has been too slack to have any reserve from which to meet drafting and over-head of small jobs that one might like to do without making a charge.
>
> I feel my bill was a very reasonable one under the circumstances and regret you evidently do not agree with me.
>
> > Very sincerely yours (October 17, 1944, Okie Papers)

This is the final letter in the Behrend file, and although Mrs. Behrend paid the bill a month later, it seems an unfortunate way to end a relationship that had begun nearly thirteen years earlier. It is made even more regrettable by the fact that Okie would suffer a tragic death fourteen months later. A *New York Times* article of December 28, 1945, notes, "R. Brognard Okie, architect, who restored William Penn's historic home, Pennsbury, was killed today in an automobile accident two miles south of West Chester. He was 70 years old" (*New York Times* 1945). Okie's son, Charles, was driving and was seriously injured. Charles would recuperate to carry on the architectural practice that his father had begun, but the chapter had closed on the correspondence between Mary Behrend and Brognard Okie.

Two weeks after Okie's death, the Philadelphia chapter of the American Institute of Architects passed a resolution in his honor, and it gives an indication of the high esteem in which he was held by his architectural colleagues. It reads in part, "Brognard Okie was a true artist. . . . Inspired by the sturdy farm houses of southeastern Pennsylvania, which he knew so well, his interpretation and his selection displayed the hand of a master. He will be best remembered as a designer of American architecture. At a time when public awareness of our rich legacy of native art was but beginning, his efforts did much to popularize and increase the growing interest in traditional American culture. This is his real monument" (Senseman et al. 1946).

CHAPTER EIGHT

A New Beginning and Lasting Legacy

In 1948, Mrs. Behrend gave Glenhill Farm and all the property to the Pennsylvania State University for the creation of a new campus. The post–World War II years were a time of great expansion in higher education, and Penn State was interested in adding a permanent campus in Erie. Mrs. Behrend gave the property as a memorial to Mr. Behrend, citing his love of education in her ceremonial speech at the college's dedication (Lane 1998, 36). The Behrend name remains as a tribute to both Mary and Ernst. Penn State Erie, the Behrend College, has grown and prospered with an enrollment of more than four thousand students and a campus of more than seven hundred acres.

The conversion of the family estate for use as a college over the course of many decades has resulted in considerable modification to the Okie-designed buildings, yet the original charm of the "Pennsylvania farm tradition" has, for the most part, been preserved. All the Okie-designed construction near Glenhill Farmhouse remains largely intact, including the main residence, garage, shelter shed, and bathhouse. Okie-altered buildings also remain; these are the farmer's office and the small barn. Several outlying buildings, all of which were at a considerable distance from the main residence and had been Okie-designed alterations to existing buildings, have been removed or demolished, including the Schley residence and garage and the house referred to as the "small house on Jordan Road."

College dedicated. In the fall of 1948, this dedication ceremony marked the transition of the Glenhill estate to a college campus. Held on the west side of Glenhill, Mrs. Behrend and Harriet (each wearing a hat) are seen seated on the left side of the dais. (Courtesy Penn State Behrend Archives.)

Generally, the exteriors look much like they did in 1934. Exceptions to this are the shelter shed, which has had its open west side enclosed, and the farmer's office, the garage, and the small barn, which have had some modifications to their doors, entryways, or facades. Numerous college buildings have been constructed over the years, including some near the core of original Glenhill buildings, and without question, these detract from Okie's design. Interiors have also been modified as the buildings have been converted to accommodate academic offices. The bathhouse and swimming pool remain as they were, although they are no longer in active use. Much of the interior of the Glenhill Farmhouse is largely unchanged. The building that most resembles its 1933 appearance—both inside and out—is the chapel across the creek in the Wintergreen Gorge Cemetery. In all, the campus core presents a mix of original design and

Students in the small barn. This early college photograph shows students gathered in the small barn. Okie's fireplace is prominent. (Courtesy Penn State Behrend Archives.)

alteration, probably an inevitable result of institutional ownership over many years.

The Behrends' interest in landscaping and gardening has been maintained and advanced by the college. Mature trees, shrubs, and other plantings surround the buildings and enhance the property's appearance to a much greater degree than when the estate was new. In recent years, the college achieved official status as an arboretum, and in 2015, a memorial garden was dedicated to honor Mrs. Behrend as a continuing tribute to her legacy. Located on the west side of the small barn, it is in the same location where she created her garden some eighty years earlier.

The makeover of an Okie-designed estate for educational, institutional, or public use is not unique to Glenhill Farm. Several other Okie-designed estates have found alternate uses in ways that have largely served to preserve much of the original architecture. Governor and Mrs. Buck's home, Buena Vista, became a conference center owned and operated by the state of Delaware. In Pennsylvania, the Appleford estate in Villanova, owned by

Mr. and Mrs. Lewis Parsons, was given to Lower Merion Township, where the grounds serve as an arboretum that is open to the public. The main house is available for weddings, conferences, and other events (Garrison 2013, 176). The property formerly known as Barclay Farm in Rosemont and owned by the McFadden family for many years has, since 1960, been owned and maintained by the Agnes Irwin School, a secondary school for girls (Morrison 2002, 52). The former Whitpain Farm of N. MacLean Seabreese, near Blue Bell, Montgomery County, provides the setting for a senior living community (Garrison 2013, 192). Near Mt. Holly, New Jersey, the Peachfield Plantation serves as a museum and the state headquarters for the National Society of Colonial Dames of America; it was a gift to that group in 1965 from Miriam Harker, who with her husband had employed Okie to design their estate at the same time he was at work on Glenhill Farm (Garrison 2013, 121). Thus Glenhill Farm can be seen as one of several estates designed by Brognard Okie that live on through their association with a cultural or educational organization.

After donating the estate, Mrs. Behrend became actively engaged with the life of the college, taking an interest in the students and in the development of the property and physical plant. Although she had relocated to Connecticut, Mrs. Behrend visited Glenhill often over the course of many years. Campus administrator Irvin Kochel recalled that her visits were highlighted by a tea with faculty and another with students, concluding that "this gave us a feeling of camaraderie that I think was rather unusual" (Kochel, n.d.). Ben Lane describes how her "nearly annual" visits were celebrated with a reception for students, often held in the large Glenhill living room: "Mrs. Behrend would talk with each student individually. She asked about their majors, their homes, and their experiences at Behrend. They sensed that she took a genuine interest in them. . . . Those who recalled these events described her manner of speaking as understated, yet enthusiastic. She evinced a deep interest in and true affection for the students gathered about her, and they showed that her great gift had indeed accomplished that for which she had hoped" (Lane 1998, 85).

The college's oldest tradition, the Hanging of the Greens, dates to 1948. In early December each year since then, a candlelight service has been held in the chapel, led by college students, in memory of the Behrend family.

Mrs. Behrend and students. This photograph documents one of Mrs. Behrend's numerous visits to the campus, during which she met with students. (Courtesy Penn State Behrend Archives.)

Chapel interior. Taken at the time of the 2016 "Hanging of the Greens" celebration by the Penn State Behrend community, this photograph shows the chapel interior, virtually unchanged from 1933. The relief on the right side of the front wall is a tribute to Warren Behrend. (Photograph by RFrank Photography.)

Blue Umbrella. This oil painting by Mrs. Behrend captures a portion of the east side of Glenhill. An avid gardener, Mrs. Behrend's hollyhocks are in bloom next to the house. (Photograph by the author.)

Part of the ceremony involves placing a wreath of holiday greens on the door of the chapel crypt. At least for some years it is known that Mrs. Behrend made the wreath of greens at her home in Connecticut and had it sent to the college for the event (Lane 1998, 55). Perhaps more than any other, this tradition maintains the modern college's connection to the Behrend family. It also serves to maintain the college's connection to part of Okie's contribution of a unique chapel as part of the family estate.

Mrs. Behrend's interest in and commitment to the college was passed on not only to her daughter, Harriet, but also to Harriet's children. Harriet led a full and active life, defined in part by her interest in competitive sports. She was a nationally ranked skeet shooter and maintained a passion for golf, boating, and equestrian activities. In 1950, she was elected to the presidency of a major women's organization in the New York metropolitan area—the Women's Metropolitan Golf Association. Twice married and twice widowed, Harriet was the mother of two sons, Richard Sayre and William Sayre, from her marriage to her first husband, Caryl Sayre. Harriet was a friend and donor to the college, and as of this writing, Richard and William Sayre serve on the college advisory board and as key supporters of the college archives, whereby they maintain an interest in the development and advancement of the Behrend Family and Hammermill Paper Company collections housed therein.

Mary Behrend died in 1976 at the age of ninety-seven. Ten years later, her daughter, Harriet, died at age seventy-five. The legacy of the Behrend family remains alive and as strong as ever through the culture and customs of Penn State Erie, the Behrend College, where their generosity and their lives are recalled and celebrated so that all students who pass through the old fieldstone gates at the college entrance are made aware of the Behrend gift. And the core college buildings retain the essence of the Behrend's Glenhill Farm in a timeless setting designed by an important domestic architect, Brognard Okie.

Bibliography

Allaback, Sarah. 2008. *The First American Women Architects*. Urbana: University of Illinois Press.

Architectural Alumni Society. 1934. *Book of the School: Department of Architecture University of Pennsylvania 1874–1934*. Philadelphia: University of Pennsylvania Press.

Architectural Record. 1932. "The Pennsylvania Type: A Logical Development, Recent Work by Mellor & Meigs, D. Knickerbacker Boyd, Duhring, Okie & Ziegler." October 1932.

Behrend, Ernst. 1933. "The Season's Greetings." *Hammermill Bond* 15, no. 1 (December 1933): inside the front cover, one page, unnumbered.

Behrend Family Guestbook. 1932. "Glenhill 1932." Behrend Family Collection 1869–1986, Penn State Behrend Archives, Penn State University Libraries, Erie, PA.

Behrend, Mary. 1943. Letter to the Internal Revenue Service, December 18, 1943. Behrend Family Collection 1869–1986, Penn State Behrend Archives, Penn State University Libraries, Erie, PA.

———. 1958. Mrs. Behrend award speech, May 1958. Behrend Family Collection 1869–1986, Penn State Behrend Archives, Penn State University Libraries, Erie, PA.

Brown, John K. 2000. "Vauclain, Samuel Matthews." American National Biography Online. http://www.anb.org/articles/10/10-01688.html.

Carson, Thomas, and Mary Bonk, eds. 1999. "Great Depression." In *Gale Encyclopedia of U.S. Economic History*, vol. 1, 394–96. Detroit: Gale.

Classic Caddys. n.d. "History, 1920–1929." Accessed August 30, 2015. http://www.classiccaddys.com/cadillac-history/16-1920-1929.

Cortner, Richard C. 2000. "Roberts, Owen Josephus." American National Biography Online. http://www.anb.org/articles/11/11-00730.html.

Daley, Scott W. 2010. "An Engineer's Story: Ernst Behrend and the Hammermill Paper Company, the First Quarter Century." PhD diss., West Virginia University.

Dixon, Mark E. 2010. *The Hidden History of Delaware County: Untold Tales from Cobb's Creek to the Brandywine*. Charleston, SC: History Press.

Erie Cemetery. 1953. "Agreement for Perpetual Care, September 29, 1953." Behrend Family Collection 1869–1986, Penn State Behrend Archives, Penn State University Libraries, Erie, PA.

Garrison, James B. 2013. *Stone Houses: Traditional Homes of R. Brognard Okie*. New York: Rizzoli.

———. 2016. Email to the author, January 8, 2016.

———. 2017. Letter to the author, September 21, 2017.

Gebhard, David. 1987. "American Colonial Revival in the 1930s." *Winterthur Portfolio* 22, no. 2/3 (Summer 1987): 109–48. http://www.jstor.org/stable/1181112.

Goldberg, Ronald Allen. 2003. *America in the Twenties*. Syracuse, NY: Syracuse University Press.

Halsey, R. T. H., and Elizabeth Tower. 1925. *The Homes of Our Ancestors: As Shown in the American Wing of the Metropolitan Museum of Art of New York from the Beginnings of New England through the Early Days of the Republic*. Garden City, NY: Garden City Publishing.

Hammermill Bond. 1938. "Hammermill Celebrates Fortieth Anniversary." *Hammermill Bond* 18, no. 7 (July 1938).

———. 1939. "Hammermill President Lends Siple Sextant." *Hammermill Bond* 19, no. 12 (December 1939).

———. 1940. "The Man He Was." *Hammermill Bond* 20, no. 10 (October 1940).

Hart, Richard L. 2010. "Richardson Brognard Okie." Pennsylvania Center for the Book. http://pabook.libraries.psu.edu/palitmap/bios/Okie_Richardson_Brognard.html.

Hergesheimer, Joseph. 1925. *From an Old House*. New York: Alfred A. Knopf.

Ingold, Jane. 2009. "Ernest Richard Behrend." Pennsylvania Center for the Book. http://pabook.libraries.psu.edu/palitmap/bios/Behrend_Ernst.html.

———. 2010. "The Best Known Name in Paper: Hammermill." Pennsylvania Center for the Book. http://pabook2.libraries.psu.edu/palitmap/Hammermill.html.

IrwinLeighton. n.d. "Irwin and Leighton Commercial Builders." Accessed September 15, 2015. http://www.irwinleighton.com.

Jangfeldt, Bengt. 2012. *The Hero of Budapest: The Triumph and Tragedy of Raoul Wallenberg*. New York: I. B. Tauris.

Karges, Steven B. 2000. "Kohler, Walter Jodok." American National Biography Online. http://www.anb.org/articles/10/10-00941.html.

Knauer, Frank. n.d. Interview. Oral History Collection 1987–. Penn State Behrend Archives, Penn State University Libraries, Erie, PA.

Kochel, Irvin. n.d. Interview. Oral History Collection 1987–. Penn State Behrend Archives, Penn State University Libraries, Erie, PA.

Koyl, George S. 1949. "An Appreciation of the Work of Richardson Brognard Okie." *A. I. A. Journal* 12 (November 1949): 213–21.

Lane, Benjamin A. 1998. *Behrend Remembered: A Half Century of Penn State in Erie*. Erie, PA: Penn State Erie, School of Humanities and Social Sciences.

Lanier, Gabrielle M., and Bernard L. Herman. 1997. *Everyday Architecture of the Mid-Atlantic: Looking at Buildings and Landscapes*. Baltimore, MD: Johns Hopkins University Press.

Lindsay, Dale. 1943. Letter to the Internal Revenue Service, November 16, 1943. Behrend Family Collection 1869–1986, Penn State Behrend Archives, Penn State University Libraries, Erie, PA.

May, Bridget A. 1991. "Progressivism and the Colonial Revival: The Modern Colonial House, 1900–1920." *Winterthur Portfolio* 26, no. 2/3 (Summer 1991): 107–22. http://www.jstor.org/stable/1181384.

McQuillen, Michael J., and William P. Garvey. 1985. *The Best Known Name in Paper: Hammermill, a History of the Company.* Erie, PA: Hammermill Paper Company.

Morrison, William. 2002. *The Main Line: Country Houses of Philadelphia's Storied Suburb, 1870–1930.* New York: Acanthus Press.

National Register of Historic Places. n.d. "Strickland-Roberts Homestead." National Register of Historic Places—Pennsylvania, Chester County. Accessed June 13, 2018. http://www.nationalregisterofhistoricplaces.com/PA/chester/state6.html.

New York Times. 1940. "Ernst R. Behrend, Maker of Paper." September 23, 1940.

———. 1945. "R. B. Okie Is Killed in Car Collision." December 28, 1945.

———. 1955. "Owen Roberts Dies; Former Justice, 80." May 18, 1955.

———. 1965. "C. Douglass Buck, Ex-Senator Dies." January 29, 1965.

———. 1968. "Paul Siple, Polar Explorer, Dies." November 26, 1968.

Okie, R. Brognard. (1931) 1977. Introduction to *Early Domestic Architecture of Pennsylvania,* by Eleanor Raymond, unpaged. Reprint of 1931 edition. Exton, PA: Schiffer.

———. 1932. "Office Memorandum regarding Requirements for Residence of Mr. and Mrs. Ernst R. Behrend, Erie, Pennsylvania." In "Correspondence, 1900–1948, 1959," MG-303, series 303m.1, Pennsylvania State Archives, Harrisburg, PA.

Pennsylvania Historical and Museum Commission. n.d. "Pennsbury Manor." Accessed September 1, 2015. http://www.phmc.pa.gov/Museums/Historic-Homes/Pages/Pennsbury-Manor.aspx.

Raymond, Eleanor. (1931) 1977. *Early Domestic Architecture of Pennsylvania.* Reprint of 1931 edition. Exton, Pennsylvania: Schiffer.

R. Brognard Okie Architectural Papers. 1793, 1828–1949. "Architectural Drawings, 1899–1978." MG-303, series 303m.9. Pennsylvania State Archives, Harrisburg, PA.

———. "Correspondence, 1900–1948, 1959." MG-303, series 303m.1. Pennsylvania State Archives, Harrisburg, PA.

———. "Specifications and Photographs." MG-303, series 303m.2. Pennsylvania State Archives, Harrisburg, PA.

Richardson, Owen. 1932. "Map of Glenhill Farm Harborcreek Township, Erie County, Penna., Property of Ernst R. Behrend." Behrend Family Collection 1869–1986, Penn State Behrend Archives, Penn State University Libraries, Erie, PA.

Richie, Margaret Bye, John D. Milner, and Gregory D. Huber. 2005. *Stone Houses: Traditional Homes of Pennsylvania's Bucks County and Brandywine Valley.* New York: Rizzoli.

Senseman, Ronald S., Leon Brown, Edwin Bateman Morris, and Charles T. Okie. 1946. *The Residential Architecture of Richardson Brognard Okie of Philadelphia.* Washington, DC: Ronald S. Senseman.

Stachelek, Jan. 2004. "Frank Knauer . . . Still a Spring in His Steps." *The Log, Erie Yacht Club,* September–October 2004.

St. David's Episcopal Church. n.d. "Who We Are—History." Accessed September 15, 2015. http://www.stdavidschurch.org.

StratfordHall.org. 2015. "Stratford Hall." Accessed June 1, 2018. http://www.stratfordhall.org.

Tatman, Sandra L. 2018. "Okie, Richardson Brognard (1875–1945)." Philadelphia Architects and Buildings. http://www.philadelphiabuildings.org/pab/app/ar_display.cfm/91390.

Time. 1923. "Samuel Vauclain." April 21, 1923.

United States Department of Labor, Bureau of Labor Statistics. n.d. "CPI Inflation Calculator." Accessed March 15, 2016. http://stats.bls.gov/data/inflation_calculator.htm.

USA Today. 2001. "Formula Used to Calculate Wind Chill." October 30, 2001.

Wallenberg, Raoul. 1995. *Letters and Dispatches 1924–1944.* New York: Arcade.

Washington Post. 1959. "Horace Peaslee, Architect, Dies." May 19, 1959.

Wikipedia. 2018. "Duesenberg." Last modified June 2, 2018. https://wikipedia.org/wiki/Duesenberg.

Photo and Illustration Credits

JAMES B. GARRISON

Drawings by and with permission of James B. Garrison. Based on drawings from R. Brognard Okie Architectural Papers, "Architectural Drawings, 1899–1978," MG-303, series 303m.9, Pennsylvania State Archives, Harrisburg, PA. (Pages 67, 68, 69)

JAMES B. GARRISON AND RICHARD L. HART

Map of Glenhill Farm buildings. (Page 38)

LIBRARY OF CONGRESS

Photograph by Jack E. Boucher, "Stratford, State Route 215, Stratford Hall, Westmoreland County, VA," Historic American Buildings Survey, National Parks Service, Department of the Interior. From Prints and Photographs Division, Library of Congress, http://hdl.loc.gov/loc.pnp/hhh.va0982/photos.166043p, accessed October 23, 2018. (Page 44)

PENN STATE BEHREND ARCHIVES, JOHN M. LILLEY LIBRARY, ERIE, PA

Behrend College Collection
Photograph by John Fontecchio. (Page 2)
Photographs by RFrank Photography, Erie, PA. (Pages 5, 56, 58, 66, 74, 127 [bottom photo])
Unattributed. (Pages 6, 90, 124, 125, 127 [top photo])

Behrend Family Collection
Behrend Family Collection 1869–1987. (Pages 7 [left and right], 9, 33, 46 [top and bottom], 49, 50, 77, 80, 81, 82, 100, 101, 102, 105, 108, 109, 111).
Photographs by Harold Haliday Costain. Reproduced with permission of Allison Costain Kessler, daughter of Harold Haliday Costain. (Pages 54, 55 [top] 59, 60, and cover design)
Photographs by Henry E. Obermanns. (Pages 103, 104, 110)

PENNSYLVANIA STATE ARCHIVES, HARRISBURG, PA

MG-303.1 R. Brognard Okie Architectural Papers, Correspondence

Letter from Mary Behrend to Brognard Okie on the letterhead of the Arizona Biltmore, undated. (Page 28)

Clipping from *House Beautiful* magazine, May 1932. (Page 30)

Letter from Ernst Behrend to Brognard Okie on the letterhead of the Arrowhead Springs Hotel, February 3, 1933, page one of two. (Page 48)

Letter from Mary Behrend to Brognard Okie on Mrs. Behrend's East Lake Road letterhead, November 11, 1932. (Page 79)

MG-303.2 R. Brognard Okie Architectural Papers, Specifications and Photographs

Photograph, model of the Behrend residence, undated. (Page 42)

Photograph of the Behrend Chapel, Wintergreen Cemetery, Erie, PA. No identification on the photograph, undated. (Page 87)

MG-303.7 R. Brognard Okie Architectural Papers, Various Items

Photograph, portrait (profile) of Brognard Okie, undated. (Page 12)

MG-303.9 R. Brognard Okie Architectural Papers, Drawings

A drawing of a proposed design for the Behrends' main residence in a Georgian style with a stone facade, titled "North Elevation," undated. (Page 44)

A series of four architectural drawings on a single sheet, titled "Addition to the Farm Office for Mr. Ernst R. Behrend near Erie, Penna," undated. (Page 78 and cover design)

SCHIFFER PUBLISHING COMPANY

Photographs from *Early Domestic Architecture of Pennsylvania*, by Eleanor Raymond, 1977 reprint edition, reproduced with permission of Schiffer Publishing Company, Atglen, PA. (Page 72)

ST. DAVID'S CHURCH

Photograph reproduced with permission of St. David's Church, Wayne, PA. (Page 87)

Acknowledgments

The author would like to express his appreciation to James B. Garrison, architect and Okie scholar, for his interest and invaluable suggestions. Mr. Garrison's foreword and drawings of the Glenhill residence add greatly to this volume. Allison Costain Kessler, daughter of Harold Haliday Costain, graciously gave permission to reproduce her father's 1936 photographs of Glenhill Farm. Christine Palattella, Office of Strategic Communications, Penn State Behrend, provided assistance with college photographs. The photograph of St. David's Episcopal Church, Wayne, Pennsylvania, was made available by Lauren Machowski, the church's director of communications. Colleagues at the John M. Lilley Library, Penn State Behrend, were most helpful. Of special note, Jane Ingold, librarian and archivist, provided easy access to archival materials and expert knowledge of the Behrend family. Finally, Christine Avery of the Penn State University Libraries saw value in the project at the earliest stages and served as a much-needed sounding board and friendly editor; her help and interest are gratefully acknowledged.

About the Author

Richard L. Hart enjoyed a career working in college libraries, including twenty-three years as the director of the Lilley Library, Penn State Behrend, from which he retired in 2017. He holds an undergraduate degree from Ursinus College and master's degrees from Clark University and Columbia University. His PhD in library and information science was earned at the University of North Carolina, Chapel Hill. Mr. Hart resides in Westfield, New York.